Gidget - The Horse That Waited For Me

by

Vicky Kaseorg

Vicky Kaseorg

ISBN-13:978-1523330171

ISBN-10:1523330171

This is a work of fiction, based on a real horse
from the author's past. Any similarities of characters
to actual people is coincidental.

Edited by Amy Fox

Cover Painting by Vicky Kaseorg
Cover Design by Neil N. Pray

But they who wait for the Lord shall renew their strength; they shall mount up with wings like eagles; they shall run and not be weary; they shall walk and not faint. Isaiah 40:31

Vicky Kaseorg

Chapter One

The man on the phone identified himself as Mr. Banks, the owner of the fanciest horse farm in Chazak, Illinois. I could hardly believe it. Why would he be calling *me*?

We had passed it several times on our Sunday family drives. It was another mile down the road from Burton's Farm. The contrast with the farm I worked at could not be more stark.

The fences were intact, and all painted white. Regularly. Recently. The horses wore blankets in the cold, and none were covered in mud with hanging heads, or the weary, worn expressions of ancient, tired nags. The neat buildings sported bright, cheery red paint. The pastures were carpeted in grass instead of mud.

"I am Richard Banks of Heritage Farm," he said, "Perhaps you are familiar with our place?"

Familiar wouldn't be quite the right word. Green with envy. Lusting after. Drooling over.

"I think so."

"I hope it is ok for me to call you. I got your name from Fiora Heller."

I blinked. I only knew one Fiora. How or why had that *tramp* given Mr. Banks my name? How had she even known it? She had not said two words to me in the few brief times I'd seen her.

"Are you there?" Mr. Banks asked, in what must have been too long a pause.

"Uh, yes. I didn't know Fiora had my number. I don't really know her well."

"She got it from her friend, Mick. I understand you developed and lead a riding class for troubled children at Burton's Farm."

"Uh, yes."

How did he know about that?? And why would Mick give Fiora my phone number?

"One of our recent new boarders knows a child in your class. She raved about the change in that little girl."

"Fiora has a horse?" I asked.

"No, Fiora goes to school with my son. They are friends…"

I detected that it was likely Fiora and the Banks boy were more than friends, judging from the way Mr. Banks' voice tightened. I also suspected Mr. Banks was not happy about that.

I know if I had a son, I wouldn't want him within a million miles of Fiora. Fiora was trouble. I hated and mistrusted her despite the fact that Bella, my best friend, was constantly reminding me that God even loves girls who dress like whores with private body parts popping out for public viewing in clothes the size of Band-Aids. Bella, being Bella, said it in a gentler, kinder manner, but I knew that my interpretation was what she meant.

It didn't help my opinion of her that Mick, Burton's sixteen-year-old son who I'd fruitlessly pined after for five years seemed smitten by her. Even Bella acted strained in Fiora's presence, and if I didn't know the deeply religious Bella hadn't a single evil bone in her body, I would think she occasionally wanted to scratch Fiora's eyes out. I know I did.

"I had actually already heard of your class through the article in the Chazak Times," Mr. Banks added.

I gloated a bit over that. One of the moms in my *horse-ercise* class was a free-lance writer for the Times. She had written a small article in the *Community Happenings* section featuring my class. My fifteen minutes of fame. I'd particularly liked the line: *this dynamo teen is a natural with horses, and understands on a visceral level how the animal/human bond can promote healing of battered souls.*

"Fiora overheard the discussion with my boarder, and told me she knew you. She offered to get me your contact information. I would be very interested in talking with you about a job with us, starting a similar class at our farm."

I almost passed out. This could not seriously be happening.

"Did you know I am only fourteen-years-old?" I asked.

He paused.

"No. I knew you were young. That makes it an even more incredible accomplishment. I understand that you volunteer at Burton's Farm in exchange for riding privileges."

How did he know that? He was correct. I'd been volunteering at Burton's Farm since age nine. I was a hard worker and not because of any admirable character quality. I LOVED the work.

Yes, even shoveling the knee-high manure from the ramshackle stalls.

Anything I could do to ease the life of those precious horses made me happy. I didn't come by that *visceral understanding of the human/animal bond* by accident.

Besides, the perk of riding any horse I wanted in exchange for my work sweetened the deal. The most precious horse was Gidget. My horse. Well, not *technically* mine, but the one I was allowed to *call* mine as long as I volunteered at Burton's farm.

She was a flighty mare who had once busted my tail-bone in her crazy spooking at any and every unfamiliar molecule. I had spent a year and a half working with her, and she had settled considerably. I would not exactly call her safe yet, but she was *safer*.

Milly, who with Burton owned the dilapidated horse farm, was kind to me, but worried. She was not convinced Gidget would ever be a reliable mount, and the farm was not rolling in cash to keep a profit-drain who despite her thin stature, ate a lot of hay.

She was half Arabian, and beautiful, unlike the other old nags at the farm. And she had produced one gorgeous filly already who was immediately sold. She was pregnant again, and since the foal was promised to Mick, would certainly not be sold until the foal was weaned.

However, Burton could (and likely would) sell her when her maternal duties ended with this foal. I'd give anything to buy her but unless some millionaire dropped a bundle of money down my chimney, that was not happening.

"Fiora is hoping to do the same volunteer arrangement there," Mr. Banks said, as though he'd heard my unspoken musings.

"Why doesn't she volunteer at your place?" I blurted. I knew it was none of my business, but if I had the choice, I sure wouldn't choose Burton's Farm over the fancy Banks' farm. She obviously had a connection to the Banks. Why didn't she take advantage of that?

Besides, I would do anything to remove her from Burton's Farm, and Mick. Thus far, she had only appeared a handful of times at the farm. That was enough for me. Mostly, I ignored the few other teen volunteers, except Mick and Bella. However, Fiora was hard to ignore. You could almost feel the heat of the grass sizzling where she walked.

Walked is not exactly the best word to describe her movement. Normally, hips don't swivel in a full circle like that in a typical walk. It was more like something you might see in X-rated movies. It didn't even seem anatomically possible. Mick definitely noticed, and I would be a pathological liar to say that didn't disturb me.

I knew my hopeless infatuation with Mick would never result in him thinking of me as anything more than a frizzy-haired, pea-head. Nonetheless, I cared that Mick would not tumble headlong into an abyss, and there was no doubt that is where any contact with Fiora would result.

I hoped she'd realize Burton's Farm was a decrepit, nasty place with flea-bag horses, and would not return.

"We…felt it best not to encourage she spend too much time with our son," Mr. Banks explained.

Ah. So Mr. Banks shared my feelings.

"Also," he quickly added, "We don't use teen volunteers. We hire professional horse people to run the farm."

Hmmm. Why was he calling me then?

"When I heard about your class, I thought it was a brilliant idea, and one I would love to implement at our farm. I didn't realize you were not yet sixteen."

That meant of course that I was not of legal working age, and could not be employed. The momentary illusion of horse-heaven opening to me shattered.

"Would you consider a similar arrangement as you have with Burton's Farm?"

"What do you mean?" I asked.

"We could possibly offer you riding privileges in exchange for you helping us develop the class."

Riding privileges! With those gleaming, trim young horses that were so valuable that they wore blankets in the cold, and each one had a stall in the cheerful red barn with sparkling white shutters?

It didn't even occur to me to consider that I would be a traitor to Burton and Milly, undercutting their business. I didn't even think about what it might mean to my favorite horse Gidget if I were to volunteer at another farm. All I thought about at that moment were the fancy horses, spotless farmyard, and manicured trails at Heritage Farm.

I didn't pause even a moment.

"Yes! I would definitely consider that."

"Wonderful! Over the summer we use our horses for trail rides, but are considering the program for the winter months when we can't run our trails."

That made sense. It is what Burton did as well.

"Could you come some afternoon this week? I can show you our farm and we could discuss our plans."

I thought quickly. In the back of my mind, it occurred to me that I didn't want Milly to know about this. I was one of her key trail guides in the summer. Mick and I were her two most reliable workers. Mick was *forced* to do trail leading, and I *loved* doing it. My absence, even for one afternoon, would be hard on Milly.

"Could I come Sunday?" I asked. Sunday was the one afternoon I didn't go to Burton's Farm. My family always went on family drives on Sunday afternoons. I knew my folks would understand if I missed one outing. Half the time, I wasn't even sure they remembered they *had* a second daughter. With five kids, one more or less didn't matter.

"That will be fine," Mr. Banks said, "Maybe around one?"

"OK. Thank you. See you then."

As soon as I hung up, I felt awash with conflicting emotions, like waves crashing against each other. I was elated with the idea of working at that fancy farm with those gorgeous horses. How could anyone *want* any skill I had to offer? My tiny head puffed to immense proportions.

But what about Gidget?

I certainly would not leave Gidget. I would have to find a way to volunteer at both farms. The class would only be once a week. One day a week I could work at Heritage Farm, and the rest of the week at Burton's.

I know you are probably thinking it was totally unrealistic that the fancy farm that only hired professional horse people would stoop to offer work, even volunteer work, to a fourteen-year-old totally unprofessional horse person. That was my first thought as well. However, this was the 1960s when no one was doing any kind of formal work with horse 'therapy' for depressed kids. No one but me.

I knew that, because I had spent hours researching it at the Chazak Community Library. There was a movement, mostly in Europe, called 'hippotherapy' but it focused on people with physical disabilities and the benefits of riding.

I chanced upon the idea of helping depressed kids mostly because of the little sister of my best friend, Bella. Her sister, Maria, was five-years-old when I met her, and so depressed over the recent death of their mom from cancer that she never even smiled. My horse (and remember, I use the word *my* loosely…she was a horse I wanted desperately but didn't own), fell in love with Maria, and the feeling was mutual. Maria was happy when she was around Gidget. It didn't take a genius to figure out that Maria was not the only depressed little kid on earth. There were waaaaay more depressed kids than I had even imagined.

I found exercises from researching the hippotherapy groups, and adapted them so they would work with little kids on old, plodding horses. Those were the only kinds of horses at Burton's Farm. That was actually a good thing because even depressed children were in little danger of the horses running away with them.

Like I said, genius was not necessary to do all this for sure, or I would not have accomplished it. However, I spent a lot of time developing a whole season worth of exercises, and had been surprisingly successful. It didn't take long before we had two full classes of sad kids getting happier.

Mr. Banks could probably have ordered one of his professional horse people to figure out how to run a class. For whatever reason, he must have decided that he could benefit from a proven track record even if it was developed by a teenager. It never crossed my mind that he might be trying to drive Burton's Farm off the face of the map, or perhaps had an even more sinister motive. I would never have agreed to meet with him if it had.

Chapter Two

"You are doing *what*?" Bella cried.

This was not the response I expected at all. Bella was a gentle, gorgeous, kind-hearted Goddess. She was one of the few people I knew who read the Bible every day, and then tried to practice at least one thing God had taught her each time. If she wasn't perfect, I still hadn't found the flaw.

"How could you even think of leaving Gidget? What will Maria do without your class?"

"I won't leave Gidget or the horse-ercise class at Burton's!" I said, "I will just work at Heritage Farm one day a week."

Bella took a deep breath, considering that. "Have you told Milly yet?"

"No. I don't think I will. I'm hoping to do the class at Heritage on Sundays so it won't affect Milly at all."

"Why wouldn't you tell Milly then?" Bella asked.

I loved Bella, but sometimes I hated her questions. She never accused me of anything, but her questions were like living parasites.

They had a way of wiggling into my brain, and nibbling my conscience. I often didn't (couldn't) answer them.

Bella waited, a patient, somewhat sorrowful look on her face. Maria dashed in at that moment, and fortunately took the heat off me.

"I'm ready!" she said.

"Nice boots," I said. She had gotten them for her seventh birthday. I always wanted real cowboy boots, but being one of five kids, all I got were hand-me-downs from my older sister. The last thing my horse-hating sister would be wearing would be cowboy boots. All my deep-seated psychological problems were courtesy of Wendy. As was my lack of cowboy boots.

We were all about to be on our way to Burton's Farm. I would be working with Gidget and her weanling filly, Trinity. Maria's best friend, Tara, was the new owner of Trinity. Tara's dad, Dr.Creola, was a veterinarian, and paid me to work with Trinity each day. She was only six-months-old now, but the goal was to break her to ride.

For now, we worked on halter skills, and were just starting work on a lunge line. Tara would meet us at the farm, as she did every Saturday. I helped her work with Trinity on the training techniques I'd practiced over the week. It still astounded me that Dr. Creola employed me to do this. As I mentioned before, I was hardly a professional horse trainer.

Gidget- the Horse That Waited For Me

I was socking that money away each week with the impossible dream of one day buying Gidget. At the rate I was going, I would have enough money to buy her by the time I was 107-years-old.

Since Gidget and Maria had a special bond, I often used Maria to help Gidget overcome her fearful response to new things. Gidget had come such a long way, that Milly thought I could try leading a trail soon with her. She had told me that this particular Saturday, Mick would lead the trail, but she would allow me to be the follower on Gidget. The follower's job was to mop up any trail riders who fell off their horses. That didn't happen much, but when it did, they were usually not skilled enough to get back on by themselves.

This day was a special one as well because Bella was starting horseback lessons. It had been a year since she had begun volunteering at the farm, but she was frightened of getting on the horses. It took me a whole year to talk her into letting me teach her. Finally, she agreed, telling me that God had numbered all her days already, and if she was not meant to survive horseback riding, she was ok with it. *God knew best.*

Bella and I did not see eye to eye on God. I was willing to admit there *might* be a God, but was not sold on the idea. Frankly, the whole idea of God creeped me out a little. Nonetheless, in the dark at night, I prayed *just in case.* If there was a God, I was a little worried He might appear. If He did that in the middle of the night, I would die of fright for sure. I figured praying hedged my bets, and protected me in the unlikely chance He showed up.

On the other hand, there were many good reasons to suspect there could not be a God. For example, if there was a God, why were there so many useless, tormenting creatures like horse-flies? In my opinion, any God worth believing in would never have created them.

At any rate, Bella didn't hold my lack of faith against me. She didn't even laugh at me when I told her about my fears at night. She assured me God would not pop out like the Bogey-man to try to give me a heart attack. She was forever pointing out that God loved me and wanted nothing more than for me to trust Him and love Him back. That idea was as alien to me as loving a moonbeam. How could someone love what one couldn't grasp?

Now Gidget was another matter. She was something I could, and fervently *did* love. I had an uncanny propensity for loving unattainable things. Joe, my first horse at Burton's Farm was the meanest, crankiest, ugliest horse there, and no one could ride him. So when I was given the choice of a horse to ride in exchange for my work, guess who I chose? Joe. It worked out since Joe loved me back, until the day he died. That was the saddest day of my life and I don't want to talk about it.

Then there was Mick. Mick, two years older than me, had hated me from the moment he saw me when I was only nine-years-old and shyer than a milkweed pod. He pummeled me with a constant barrage of insults. So naturally, I worshiped him.

Gidget- the Horse That Waited For Me

I know. The deep rooted psychological reasons for *that* could be a book in itself. And now, at age fourteen, I still loved him. He never encouraged it in any way, and that seemed to be all the encouragement I needed.

Then there was Gidget. After Joe's death, I was again allowed to choose any horse on the farm to ride in exchange for my work there. Did I choose a nice, calm, stable, gentle horse within my meager riding capabilities? Nope. I chose the second least favorite horse on the farm after Joe. Gidget was young, only green-broke, and dangerously spookish. She shied at everything, and was afraid of everything. No one wanted to ride her, and no one did, until I came along.

She had nearly killed me a few times. All by accident. She was not mean. Just *crazy* flighty. She liked me, but not enough to overcome her irrational fears. Over the past year and a half, we had made progress.

I discovered that she inexplicably calmed when I sang to her. That was my secret training technique. She was an old-fashioned horse and preferred music from before the 1960s. That was fine, since that was the only music I knew. The old MGM musicals were my favorite, and apparently Gidget's as well.

"Who will Bella ride?" Maria asked, as we walked along the busy Narroway highway.

"I think Skippy would be the best first horse for you to try," I suggested.

"Skippy!" Maria said, "But Skippy is just a pony!"

"Perfect," Bella said, smiling at me.

"Even I am too big for Skippy," Maria said.

"That's because you are brave," Bella said, squeezing Maria's hand. Maria nodded solemnly.

Bella was right. Maria *was* brave. She had survived her mother's death. I could not think of anything requiring more courage from a child. Tara was waiting for us as we rounded the corner of the barn and entered the dusty yard. Trail horses were already being lined up and groomed by the other volunteers.

Peeper, Mick's little sister, grabbed Maria's hand and asked if she and Tara could come help her feed the pigs. Bella nodded, and the three little girls dashed off.

Mick was saddling a trail horse, but when he saw us, more specifically *Bella*, he cinched it quickly, and raced over to us. He was as hopelessly in love with Bella as I was with him.

Unless Fiora was around. I don't think he loved Fiora like he loved Bella, but he was pretty magnetized by her anatomically impossible hip swirls clad in her impossibly short shorts.

"Hi Bella!" he said. I waited for him to notice me, but as usual, in vain.

Bella never let me be dismissed like that.

"Hi Mick! Did you know Vicky is teaching me to ride today? Isn't she great!?"

Mick cast a quick look in my direction, caught in an awkward situation. He could hardly say what he was thinking which was, *no she is a hay-headed turd.* On the other hand, if he said *yes, she's wonderful*, he risked undoing five years of disdain.

To be fair, he had warmed to me a little in the past year. I had unwittingly uncovered the death several years earlier of his older brother. Mick had carried the grief and guilt of racing his brother in the forbidden pasture on a newly trained colt. The horses collided and Mick's brother was thrown from the horse, snapping his neck and dying instantly. For some reason, Mick confided in me the terrible secret grief and guilt over his brother's death. On occasion, since that time, he treated me almost as a fellow human.

"I can help," Mick said, skirting the need to acknowledge how great I was or wasn't.

"No, you can't," Milly said, approaching us with another saddle in hand. "You are leading the next trail, and the horses need to be tacked in fifteen minutes." Mick scowled, but returned to the line of trail horses. Milly smiled at us. "Hi Bella. If you and Vicky want to follow the trail, I am sure Skippy will be fine."

I was not so sure. My first time on Skippy, Milly had smacked Skippy's bottom and sent me off after the trail riders. I had ended up clinging to Skippy's belly, upside down, before thudding to the hard ground.

Besides, I had ridden Gidget on the trail by myself several times, and she had done well. However, she had not yet been accompanying the other trail horses. I wasn't certain she would be fine under those conditions.

"Ok," Bella said, to my surprise.

I darted a look at her.

"I'll keep an eye on the girls till you get back," Milly said.

As she headed over to the trail horse to saddle him, I grabbed Bella's arm. "I thought you were afraid."

"Yea though I walk through the valley of death, I will fear no evil, for thou art with me."

Bella was always doing that, quoting scripture. I had half the Bible memorized just by being her friend for almost two years now.

"I art with you," I said, "but I can't guarantee my horse will be calm. You might be on your own."

"Not *thou*, as in you. *Thou* as in God."

"I hope God is good with ponies," I said.

We stopped off at the tack room for Skippy's bridle and Gidget's hackamore.

"I'll give you a quick lesson in the pasture," I said.

Gidget came trotting over as soon as she saw me. I bridled her, and nuzzled my cheek against hers. Her filly, who was almost Gidget's size now, also approached, looking for my regular offering of carrots. I fed both of them, and then we headed over to Skippy who stood near old Joe's favorite tree.

Skippy was the tamest pony at the farm. He was old, and had weathered many new riders. He was also tiny. Bella bridled him, after giving him a carrot.

She had helped the *horse-ercise class* riders mount their horses enough times that she was familiar with the drill. From the beginning, she had been my assistant with the horse-ercise class I developed. She put her bent knee in my hands and I helped shove her on Skippy's back. It was not at all hard, since he was so small. Her feet nearly touched the ground as she straddled him.

As she gathered the reins, she laughed.

"It's like being in the Flintstone's car," she said, "I can almost just walk myself, my feet are so close to the ground! Are you sure he will be okay?"

"I'm sure," I said, chuckling, "But if you have to fall, at least you don't have far to go."

"I'm not even scared!" She beamed at me.

"You know how to neck rein," I said, "so just follow me and Gidget." I clambered atop Gidget, hoisting myself up by grabbing her mane and flopping across her back. Despite all the years of riding, I was still never graceful in that maneuver. It remained a favorite source of Mick's taunts.

Fortunately, he was busy saddling the trail horses and didn't notice. As we started towards the barn, Bella shrieked.

"Sorry!" she said quickly. She clutched Skippy's mane.

"You're doing great!" I assured her. "This is as hard as it gets."

That was not quite true. There was a short segment on the trail when we would trot. Trotting is much bouncier than a walk, and novice riders have a hard time 'melting' into the bounce. It can be pretty jarring until one learns to relax the pelvis and roll with the movement.

We could walk during that portion of the ride. I would let Bella know when we reached that junction. No use scaring her now. We dismounted at the barn.

"See," I said, "Was it fun?"

"Yes," Bella answered, "but what about when we trot?"

I could never get anything past Bella.

"You don't have to trot. The other horses don't go very fast, and the trotting portion isn't very long."

"I want to trot. I've been thinking that I need to stop being afraid. After all this time at the farm, it's about time I confront my fears."

We led our horses through the barn and out to the yard, where trail riders were already mounting their horses with assistance from Milly and the other teen volunteers. Mick was astride the peppiest of the old horses, which wasn't saying much. Gidget and her filly were the only horses at the farm under twenty-five–years-old.

"You're coming with me?" he asked. His smile widened, teeth gleaming like a jackal at Bella.

She nodded, looking nervous now.

"Don't be afraid," Mick said, "I'll help you."

"Head out Mick," Milly said. He snatched his eyes off Bella, and led the way to the trail head. One by one, the old nags filed after him, with their nervous riders clutching the saddle horns.

Milly took a hold of Skippy's reins under his chin, and as she led him to the trail head, gave much the same advice as she had given me those long years ago.

"Kick him when you want to go. Pull back when you want to stop. That's all there is to it."

I nodded to Bella, and brought up the rear. I noticed her knuckles were white, clutching Skippy's mane. Mick looked back several times. He ignored the trail riders in his charge, but called back often to Bella.

"You're doing great, Bella. You are a natural."

Even Bella knew that was crazy talk, fueled by hormones.

"I am a natural blonde. That's the only natural part of me on a horse," she said to me.

I laughed. "It will feel natural after you have done it a few times."

It was a perfect day to be on a horse. Winters in Chazak are terrible, and no one in their right mind wants to live through an Illinois winter. However, payback time comes in the summer. The trees were deep green and leafy, birds and butterflies were flitting in and out of the shadows, and fluffy clouds dotted the sky. It was warm, but not too hot. The sun felt like warm lotion oozing over my arms.

Gidget was relaxed. She was a few months pregnant with her second foal, and the extra weight and maternal hormones seemed to center her. Some mares get irritable when they are pregnant, but not Gidget. Motherhood calmed her. Bella suggested that it was I who was calmer, more confident, and my attitude was what was changing Gidget.

Predictably, she supported that with a Bible verse.

"You and Gidget are becoming of one mind," she said, "The Bible says, *Complete my joy by being of the same mind, having the same love, being in full accord and of one mind.*"

"Hmmm. How can you tell?"

"I know the signs." She didn't expand upon that enigmatic statement. I didn't know if we were of one mind, but my joy was being completed by having a horse that didn't toss me off every few minutes shying at unseen enemies.

We plodded along, mostly in silence. I could tell Bella was slowly adjusting, even enjoying the ride. As usual, we were being lulled by a false sense of security. You just never can plan for the unexpected.

Up at the front of the trail line, I saw a flash of bright red, as a figure emerged from the forest. A scantily clad girl in scarlet clothes the size of Band-Aids. Mick's horse slammed to a halt.

Fiora! What was she doing on the trail?

The other trail horses dropped their heads to graze while Mick and Fiora chatted. I was too far back to hear what they were saying, but judging from the seductive look on Fiora's face, they were not exchanging crock-pot recipes.

"What's she doing here?" Bella asked me.

My guess was she was posing for a Playboy magazine spread, based on the way she was dressed. I didn't say that because I didn't have time. She stepped back, and Mick spurred his poor old horse, whose head shot up and he catapulted forward. The sudden movement startled the rest of the trail horses who all jerked the reins from their unsuspecting rider's hands as they leaped after Mick's horse.

Horses are herd animals. When one horse signals danger, the others follow. Mick knew better than to dash forward so suddenly with novice trail riders behind him. I have no idea what Fiora said to him, but she was laughing and clapping, so I suspect it was some sort of dare to wake those old nags up.

I was savvy enough with Gidget's temperament to have already gathered my reins and anticipated she would bolt. She danced in place, but didn't thunder off like everyone else. Poor Bella was not so lucky. Skippy, though good-natured and normally reliable, shot off after the herd.

At this point, I had no choice. I had to follow and do my best to help bring the group under control. I had no real idea of how I would manage that, especially since at that point, Gidget took matters in her own hooves. Her brief control came to a screeching halt, and she catapulted after Skippy.

As we thundered by Fiora, she sneered at me, doubled over in laughter. If there was a God I hoped He was watching and seriously considering smiting her.

Half the riders tumbled off, including Bella. I managed to stop Gidget and jumped off, holding tightly to her reins. It was pretty amazing that Gidget was the calmest horse of that geriatric crowd.

Bella had the wind knocked out of her, but she stood up and assured me she was fine when I reached her. We slowly collected the other fallen riders, and all walked along the trail, in the dust of the receding stampede.

"What a miracle," Bella said, between gasps, as we reached the last dumped rider. I looked at her, stupefied.

"Miracle?"

"No one was hurt," she said. "I told you God numbers our days."

"He better refund my money too," one of the fallen riders said.

Chapter Three

She was right too. No one was hurt, unless you counted Mick. When Burton heard the story, he pulled out his belt, but Bella looked straight at him with a pleading look. Slowly, Burton lowered the strap. I don't know if Mick got walloped after we were out of sight or not. However, Burton was not known for 'sparing the rod.'

When I was working with Trinity and Tara, Mick came across the field and stood nearby watching. For some inexplicable reason, he appeared to want to talk to me. I helped Tara remove Trinity's halter, and she scampered off to find Peeper. Gidget stood next to me, and rubbed her head against my belly. She knew I was a sucker for that show of affection. I dug into my pocketful of carrot pieces and offered one to her. Mick came closer.

"Why did you do that, Mick?" I asked.

"Do what? Look like a movie star? It just happens."

"No, take off like that during the trail ride."

"The riders like to go fast."

"Mick, you knew half of them would fall off. Including Bella."

He hung his head, "I *did* feel bad about Bella."

"It was stupid." I glared at him.

"I didn't mean to hurt Bella," he said.

"You were showing off to Fiora," I snapped angrily. "Why?"

"Have you *seen* Fiora?" he asked.

I turned away, disgusted. I knew I was never going to be a girl boys slathered over, but there was a line I would not cross to be an object of attention. It was about a thousand miles from the line Fiora apparently drew.

"Look, I'm sorry. I shouldn't have done that. I didn't think those old nags would do more than trot."

"You *know* horses better than anyone, Mick. How could you not know they would act like that? For sure you knew Gidget would flip." My eyes watered unexpectedly. Ah. I had not really known till that moment that I had felt a personal affront.

Mick was silent, gazing at me.

"That's what Dad said," he said finally. "And then he threatened to take Gidget's foal from me."

"It serves you right," I said, brushing the tears away as unobtrusively as I could.

"He said if I apologized to you he would reconsider."

I shook my head in disgust. That was the only reason he had shown up to express regret.

"Not that that's the only reason I'm apologizing," he added quickly.

I couldn't imagine any other *sincere* reason so I picked up the tack I'd brought out to lunge Trinity with, and started back to the barn.

"He's making me help him with a new farrier job," Mick said, falling in beside me.

I didn't say anything. Maybe Mick did feel some measure of guilt. I couldn't imagine why he didn't disappear after the forced apology.

"Fiora told me something about you," he said.

I stopped.

"I figured she was lying…but the strange coincidence is the new farrier job is at Heritage Farm."

I bit my lip, and didn't look at him. How I hated that Fiora! It hadn't occurred to me she would mention any of my plans to Mick.

"I didn't know that was why she wanted your phone number," he said, "I didn't think you would be a traitor."

I spun around. "I am not being a traitor! I will be at Burton's Farm just as much as always. I am just talking to Mr. Banks about helping more sad children. What's so bad about that?"

"I don't know…" Mick said slowly, "Why didn't you mention it to me then?"

"In case you haven't noticed, you are not Mr. Congeniality to me," I said.

I stomped off, while Mick watched me. Now I had no choice but to tell Milly. Mick would if I didn't, and it would make me look guilty. *Which I wasn't.*

Milly was in the barn, filling feed buckets for the goats and pigs.

"Milly, do you know about Heritage Farms?" I asked.

She looked up from measuring the grain.

"Yes. Burton just got a call for some work with them. Fancy place down the highway. They just won some big show with a new gaited horse they paid more money for than our farm is worth." I knew that didn't likely represent astronomical sums, but kept that observation to myself.

Nonetheless, she did not sound like she liked Heritage Farm.

"In fact, last winter when half our boarders left because we didn't have the indoor arena yet, that's where they went. It almost seemed like they were trying to run us out of business. Not that it would take much."

She was definitely not making full disclosure easy. I opened my mouth to spurt out the details of my talk with Mr. Banks when she added, "And then they started a trail riding program this summer. They are more expensive than us, but this summer's business is cut by a third of last summer's. Mick's stunt today won't help."

I snapped my mouth shut.

"Why do you ask about them?" she said.

Bella and I had a discussion a few days ago that popped into my head at that moment. She told me there are constant opportunities before us that are crossroads in life. We can make the choice to do good or not. We can listen to our conscience, which she called the Holy Spirit, or can ignore it. She told me the more we ignore it, the less we hear it.

"Every choice moves us in one direction or another," she had said.

"Aren't some choices just neutral?" I had asked, "Like whether to have orange juice or apple juice for breakfast?"

She'd laughed, flipping her stunning golden hair over her shoulder. "Yes, I guess a few are. But every time you make a choice for something, you are making a choice to reject something else. What if your little sister loves apple juice and there is only one serving left? Then if you choose apple juice, you are making a choice for selfishness."

"Not necessarily," I'd argued, "I am helping promote survival of the fittest."

Bella smiled at me, and didn't say anything else. She knew she'd made her point and arguing was not her style.

I snapped back to my discussion with Milly. "Mick said he was going to help Burton with a farrier job there. Does that bother you that *they* are going to help Heritage Farm?"

"No," she said, "I hope it sparks some responsibility in Mick. And Lord knows we need the money. There is no crime in working to support ourselves."

She looked at me, as though she knew something else was on my mind. I just couldn't tell her. Maybe she would find out eventually, but I lost courage.

"See you Monday," I said instead.

I have to admit that the next day, I ran as fast as I could past Burton's Farm on my way to Heritage Farm. Fortunately, no one was in the yard to see me except Marmaduke, the watch dog. He barked, and wagged his tail.

The driveway into Heritage Farm was lined with big willow trees. Flanking the trees were spotless white fences. A couple of stunning horses grazed in the nearby pasture. Their coats were shiny and clearly groomed every day. Unlike Burton's driveway of muddy ruts and patches of gravel, this one was paved all the way into the barn yard.

Mr. Banks was standing just inside an immense red barn. Not a speck of manure was in sight. What did they do with it? If you own horses, guaranteed there is manure. Even fancy horses have to poop.

There were four aisles off the main room of the barn, and they were filled with impressive box stalls. Gleaming steel bars covered each door. Nearly every one was filled with a horse, which surprised me. On such a gorgeous day, Burton's horses would all be in the pasture looking for the nonexistent grass. And Heritage Farm pastures *had* grass.

Mr. Banks shook my hand.

"Pleasure to meet you, Vicky!"

"Um. You too."

"First let me show you around a little and then we can talk about the class."

"OK."

I was overwhelmed. Not that I have a huge command of my vocal cords around most people in any situation, but when I feel out of my element, the mute factor increases a million percent.

Above every stall door was a brass nameplate. The horses had fancy names like Excalibur, Stoneybrook III, Admiralty, and the like. Mr. Banks was rattling off their lineage, as though I understood the importance. I did understand that if these horses were people, they would have descended from royalty.

"This is our latest addition," Mr. Banks said, pausing in front of a stall that contained a dark brown horse. The horse looked at me with tender big eyes. He kept shifting the weight on his front hooves. I glanced down. The strangest shoes were on his hooves. They were huge with a strap crossed over the top of his hooves, probably to hold them on. His pasterns were wrapped in white tape. Heavy chains circled his fetlocks. His eyes looked pained.

"This is our champion Tennessee Walking Horse," Mr. Banks said, "Just won a big show in Knoxville last week."

"What's his name?" I asked. I wanted to reach in and touch his muzzle. He looked lonely.

"Sheridan."

"What are those things on his hooves?"

"Our trainer uses those special shoes to help his gait. Walking Horses are known for their high stepping gait. The shoes help prepare them for the shows."

I had seen Tennessee Walking Horses on television. They were a bit of a rage since Elvis Presley owned some. I'd seen news clips of him and his gorgeous wife Priscilla riding them.

"They lift their legs like that naturally?" I asked.

"Yes," Mr. Banks said, "Some more than others. Sheridan has what we call a 'big lick.' Mighty impressive."

"Does he wear those chains all the time?"

"No, the trainer is about to work with him. They come off when he's done."

"They look heavy."

Mr. Banks frowned at me. He seemed annoyed but I couldn't help myself. The shoes and chains looked heavy and uncomfortable.

"A horse weighs a thousand pounds. He's barely going to notice that little chain," Mr. Banks said.

We moved on, and Mr. Banks took me to the indoor riding arena. It was lined with bleachers, well lit, and he added, "heated in the winter." I suspected it was not built with the wood from tumbled down sheds like Burton's indoor arena.

"This is where you would be running your class."

I was perplexed. Why would someone with all this wealth and fancy horses be interested in hiring a kid like me to run a program? It made no sense at all.

Mr. Banks led me next to a back pasture where a small herd gathered that looked a little more like Burton's horses. They were not the young, gleaming, flashy horses that were inside the barn. (Don't think they were the mud-covered, saggy old nags with an average age of thirty, like Burton's horses. They were just not quite as impressive as Mr. Banks' barn horses.)

"These are some of our retired horses," he said, "And they are very calm, and older. They are what we use for our trail rides and novice riders. They are the horses we'd use for your class. Our trainers concentrate on the show horses in the barn, so frankly, that's why we were interested in using you for the children's class. We want to give back to the community in a small way."

"Do you have people interested in the class?" I asked.

Mr. Banks didn't answer immediately. He seemed to be weighing his words carefully.

"I assume some of your students at Burton's would be interested in attending."

I startled a bit, and almost gasped. Was he really suggesting he would openly steal Milly's clients?

"Not that we would suggest that," he added quickly, "But the heated arena might be a better environment for some children. And some might want a second class. I assume you would…continue…the class at Burtons?"

I nodded. I was beginning to suspect he wanted a kid to run this program because a kid might not notice how unethical this all was beginning to sound.

"Are you paid?" he asked.

I wasn't sure if I should answer. I *was* paid, of course, but I wondered if Burton would get in trouble for paying me since I wasn't of legal employment age. While weighing how I ought to respond, he said, "We would pay you half of the fee for every child in the class. As well as letting you ride one of our horses after class."

At this point, I could not contain the question in me any longer. "Mr. Banks, this all sounds great, but I don't understand why you want *me* to do this."

"Our barn is always under scrutiny with the show horses we train, and we want the public to know that we care about how our animals benefit the community. There have been several articles in the local paper about us, and we felt this program would help show the positive contribution we can make to equitation in Chazak."

I wondered what articles had been in the paper. I was a voracious reader, but rarely bothered with the newspaper. It only had boring stories like impending nuclear holocausts, or latest death tolls in Viet Nam. Since horses were almost never mentioned, I had no interest.

A horse neighed behind us, and we turned. Sheridan, the Tennessee Walking Horse, was being led out of the barn by a tall man, with a whip in his hand. He was dressed awfully nicely for someone who works with horses. No one at Burton's Farm ever looked that neat and respectable. I instantly hated the man. I am not much of a lover of humanity in general, but something about this man hit me at a gut level with repugnance.

Sheridan was prancing, lifting his heavy front hooves to a ridiculous height. It almost looked like he was in pain. As soon as one hoof touched down, it sprang up again. They disappeared into the arena, but not before I saw the trainer strike the horse near his muzzle.

I gaped in horror. I couldn't possibly have seen what I had thought I'd seen. Why would anyone hit a show horse, or any horse, in the face? He had seemed to balk before entering the ring, but I knew smacking a balky horse often just made the problem worse.

"So what do you think?" Mr. Banks asked, "Do you have any questions?"

Yeah, why did the trainer smack that horse in the face?

"When would you want me to start?" I asked instead.

"I was hoping we could develop the program over the summer. Outline the exercises for each class, and be all ready by winter for the program to be implemented."

"Will Sunday mornings work for you?" I asked.

"We could probably make that work."

"And I don't need a horse to ride," I said, "But I'd like to be able to spend time with a horse. Like Sheridan."

Mr. Banks looked surprised. "What do you mean? I can't let you work with Sheridan. He requires special handling."

"No, I just mean groom him, feed him. Just be with him. Would that be okay?"

Mr. Banks nodded slowly. "I personally don't see any harm in that. But honestly, it is up to the trainer, and he is particular with Sheridan. I am afraid that would probably not be possible. You let me know if you change your mind and decide you want a horse to ride. Your help since you have experience doing this is very valuable to us."

As we walked through the pasture, I battled with my warring thoughts. One side of me said I should run as fast as I could from this strange offer and the trainer who I was certain was mistreating the horse. The other side of me thought that having a chance to work with such beautiful horses in such a beautiful setting would be a chance of a lifetime. Besides, maybe I could help Sheridan.

"What do you think?" he asked.

I glanced around me, at the sleek horses dotting the pasture, the lush grounds, the spotless barn. I heard a shrill neigh from the covered arena. That poor horse. "I am willing to come Sunday and go from there."

He shook my hand and walked me back to the barn. I waved and started down the long, shady driveway. It felt like coming out of a dream. None of it made sense to me despite Mr. Banks explanation. Unease settled over me, like a layer of grime.

Now I organized my thoughts. First, the trainer was cruel. No doubt about that. Secondly, that horse had been in pain. I saw it in his eyes. And fright, beneath the gentle gaze. Based on my disgust with what I had seen, I should have turned Mr. Banks down except I had the sense Sheridan was pleading with me. It was strange.

I knew nothing about Tennessee Walking Horses or how they were trained, but I knew what I had seen was not right. I didn't see any way I could possibly help the horse, but I knew I couldn't help him if I had no access to him. Maybe it was stupid, but I decided that returning Sunday was the only possible choice I could have made.

Before I returned, I knew exactly who could help me research what was going on at that farm. If there were articles in the paper, Miss Scruggs would be able to track them down. Rather than going home, I headed directly to Chazak Community Library.

Chapter Four

Miss Scruggs instantly found several articles about Heritage Farm. There was one about the newly purchased Sheridan, with the list of his wins. He was young, recently on the show circuit, but already making a name for himself locally.

The second article was a whole lot more disturbing. The trainer at Heritage Farm had been implicated in past abuse of gaited horses. He was accused of *soring,* which was the purposeful infliction of pain to the legs and hooves of a gaited horse to induce them to step with an exaggerated high gait. I had never heard of soring until that moment. My life would have been a lot happier and simpler if I had remained ignorant.

Nothing had ever been proven against the trainer, but soring was such a pervasive problem in gaited show horses that Congress passed a Horse Protection Act just that year (1970) to prevent it. I won't turn your stomach the way mine turned while reading excruciating details about what trainers did to Tennessee Walking Horses to elicit the high step. I will just summarize.

Sometimes they packed heavy weighted shoes with nails and other irritants that dug into the horse's tender sole. Sometimes they put caustic chemicals on the horse's pastern (above his hoof) and then wrapped it with tape so the chemicals burned into his skin. First they cut little scratches in his skin so the chemicals would burn into his flesh more effectively, causing more pain. Then when they worked the horse, they put chains around the pasterns that dug into the sores, and created even more pain. Sometimes they caused purposeful infection of the laminae of the hoof, setting off incredibly painful foundering. The purpose of all this torture was to get the horse to snap his feet higher off the ground so he would win shows.

"Vicky? Are you ok, honey?" Miss Scruggs stood over me, laying a hand on my shoulder.

I looked up and realized that I was dripping tears all over her newspaper article. Fortunately, it was encased in plastic. Good thinking.

"No," I whispered, and I lay my head down on the library table and sobbed all over the plastic encased article. Miss Scruggs patted my back.

Eventually, I managed to get up, gather my things, and thank Miss Scruggs. She didn't try to console me, which I appreciated. What consolation is there? I was ashamed to be human, to be a part of the species that would do such unthinkable things to an innocent creature.

Gidget- the Horse That Waited For Me

I walked home slowly, tears still cascading like the spring thaw down the valleys of my cheek. You would think that such a despicable practice would be easy to spot and put an end to. It was not.

The way trainers avoid detection is almost as cruel as the training itself. They put numbing agents and nerve blocks on the horse's pastern before a show so if inspectors check for soring, the horse doesn't flinch under their touch. The inspectors palpate the pasterns, and if the horse stands calmly, without indicating he is hurting, it is hard to accuse the trainer of soring. The trainers disguise the scars from the chemical wounds by painting the area, dusting, and blending the color of the raw skin to the hair to escape detection.

Perhaps the most heartbreaking way the trainers avoid detection is by inflicting more pain on the horse if he responds to the pain in his hooves. In essence, they are teaching the horse that unless he stoically endures the pain and stands still while inspectors examine him, he will be tortured further. I had read about 'learned helplessness' in school. This is exactly what was happening with the horses.

In training, they use *distractors* such as electric shock to the muzzle so the horse will be in more pain from the shock than the terribly painful hooves, and will learn to stand still despite the pain. When the horse lies down and refuses to get up because of the pain, they beat the horse till he stands.

I found myself at Bella's house, without any idea of how I'd gotten there. Mr. Temple answered the door, took one look at me and asked if I was all right. He ushered me in as I mutely shook my head.

"Bella!"

She came around the hall, and saw me, snot and tears dripping all over my shirt.

Without a word she came and put her arms around me. "Is it Gidget?"

I shook my head and then cried in earnest as she held me.

"It's Sheridan…."

"Who's Sheridan?"

Somehow, between hot chocolate (courtesy of Mr. Temple) and Bella stroking my frizzy hair, I managed to choke out the whole terrible story.

"How can I work there…but who will help Sheridan if I don't?"

"Do you know they are doing that awful stuff to him?" Mr. Temple asked.

"No. But his pasterns were wrapped, just like in the soring pictures I saw in the library article. And he had those big heavy shoes, and chains, and I saw the trainer hit his face."

"Maybe Dr. Creola can help," Bella suggested.

"How could any farrier assist in something like this?" Mr. Temple said.

That reminded me of Burton, and the work he would be doing that week with Mick.

"Mr. Banks called Burton to do some farrier work," I said. "Mick is going with him."

"Does Burton know about this?" Bella asked, horrified.

"I don't know. I don't think so. I don't think he has ever worked for them before, but I don't know."

Would Mick, cruel as Mick had been in the past to horses, ever be *this* cruel? Did *he* know?

"When is Burton going?" Mr. Temple said.

"Tomorrow. I read that farriers get paid a lot of money to keep quiet about what happens in these places. Sometimes the vets too. There's a lot of money in the top shows, and then the breeding status of the top winners. The poor horse." The tears returned afresh.

"We need to talk to Mick," Bella said.

I looked at her through the fountain spritzing my eyelashes. "Why?"

"He will be our spy. We need to prep him."

"I am not sure this is a good idea," Mr. Temple said.

Bella looked at her father. "We won't do anything dangerous Dad, but you wouldn't have us know about this and do nothing, would you? That is not how the Good Samaritan behaved."

He gently stroked her cheek. "You are an angel, my girl. I would not have us do nothing, but I don't think this is the place for children to be involved."

"Mr. Temple," I said, "I don't want anything to happen to that horse. Can we just talk to Burton? If I turn down the job, there will be no one there who cares watching the horse."

Bella looked at her father. "We will just talk to Mick and Burton. We won't go to Heritage Farm or anything. I promise you, Dad."

He looked from me to Bella. "I admire you both. You can talk to them, but no more. Do not go anywhere near Heritage Farm, Bella. Vicky, I can't tell you what to do, but please let your parents know before you consider working there."

I was secretly glad that I didn't have that whole God thing going on like Bella did. Any promise I made was not quite as binding. We plotted and discussed our plan, gathered our materials, and dashed out. We ran all the way to the farm.

Mick was already tossing hay bales on the flatbed for the afternoon feeding. He was surprised to see Bella, though she came more often now that summer was here.

He almost passed out with joy when she said, "Mick, we need to talk to you. Privately." His joy was shattered when he saw me tagging along.

"Vicky, don't you have some stall to make ##@$%**&^*-licking clean?" That little bit of colorful language slipped out in his excitement over Bella. Normally he squelched such language in her presence.

"Sorry!" he added quickly, "I didn't mean that the way it sounded. It is just *that* amazing to me how gosh-darn sparkling you get those stalls."

Bella had a pained look on her face but didn't comment.

"We, as in Bella *and I,* need your help," I said.

He followed us to the goat pen where no one might eavesdrop on us other than the goats. They did appear interested, all gathering and butting us for hand-outs.

The terrible story flowed out of me, draining more tears from my red eyes. Mick listened. I watched his face for signs of horror, but didn't detect nearly the degree of revulsion I'd hoped for. When I finished, Bella said, "If you and Burton are going tomorrow, we thought you could take pictures of what is in that poor horse's shoes."

In the late 60's, cameras were not super small. The most common camera was a Kodak instamatic. Mick would have to be pretty clever and quick to snap any pictures undetected. Also, we knew it was unlikely Mick had one, since Burton was not exactly rolling in money, and he quickly corroborated that.

"First, great idea. I will go rob K-mart and get a camera. Second, I don't even know what horses we're working on. I doubt it will be any prize show horse. And thirdly, will you go out with me Saturday night if I do this?"

This last question was directed to Bella. Although it's unlikely you didn't figure that out, better to clear any potential confusion immediately.

She pulled a Kodak out of her pocket, dangling it in front of him.

"Great, at least you won't have to date a thief!"

"Mick, I am not going out with you. We hoped you would help because it is the right thing to do."

"What makes you think I will be able to sneak a picture even if this *is* the horse we work on? I imagine the trainer will be right there if the horse is so valuable."

"We thought if anyone could manage, it would be you, with your sneaky personality," I said.

He nodded, not at all insulted. I knew he would consider that comment to be a compliment.

"If I succeed, then will you go out with me?"

"If you succeed, God will bless you," she said.

"Will God bless me with you going out with me?" He grinned at her. She was about to answer when who should come crunching down the gravel driveway with hips twirling like a gyroscope but Fiora!

Mick's features slackened, and his tongue almost flapped out of the side of his mouth. His eyes widened, and he absently stuffed the camera in his pocket.

"I'll see what I can do," he said, quickly springing over the fence and rushing to Fiora's side. They walked away together, back towards the trail Fiora had emerged from while Bella and I watched.

"I wonder if they are on their way to church?" I asked.

"Probably," Bella said, with a sigh. "I pray for that girl…"

"You do? What do you pray? That the earth will crack open and swallow her whole?"

"Vicky, God loves her soul as much as yours or mine."

One would think that an all-knowing Being like God would have more discernment. I didn't say that to Bella because I didn't want her to think I was mocking her faith.

The next day, I was at the farm when Burton gathered his farrier tools, whistled to Mick, and the two started off in the truck to Heritage Farm. Mick winked at me, patting his pocket.

With Mick gone, Milly asked me how I felt about leading the next trail group on Gidget. This was a huge vote of confidence! I had no idea Milly thought Gidget was reliable enough to lead a trail!

"I know the problem with the last trail was Mick's stunt, not you or Gidget. From what I could tell, you kept Gidget under control."

I nodded, eager to prove that Gidget could be a valuable contributor to the farm. "I think she is ready. She hasn't shied at all with me in months."

"It's a small group," Milly said, "Just three riders. Our business has definitely suffered since Heritage started trail rides."

Her brow creased, and she wrapped her braid around her fingers like she did when she was deep in thought. "I don't know how long we can hold out if they keep overlapping with our business."

This would be a good time to tell her about their offer of the horse-ercise class job. I should tell her then and there how I decided to turn it down. Except…I hadn't. That poor Sheridan kept hoofing his way into my head and I had the delusional sense that I could help him.

Besides, with all that money they were offering, I could almost seriously consider buying Gidget. I had no idea what Gidget might sell for, but my little savings account was slowly growing. Additionally, if I bought Gidget, I'd be helping Burton, so I wasn't *really* a Benedict Arnold by teaching the class at Heritage. I kept quiet.

When I ran out to the pasture to catch Gidget, she saw me, whinnied, and trotted to meet me. Trinity, who was off flirting with the old biddies on the other side of the pasture, raised her head and nickered but then continued exchanging gossip with Beauty. Trinity liked me, but not the way Gidget did. I think Gidget understood that I was *her* human. No one else paid Gidget any attention, not even the other horses. It was pretty clear to me that Gidget knew I was her link to safely remaining at the farm, and her only real friend.

On the other hand, it could be my carrots. She really liked my pockets perennially bulging with carrots. She nuzzled my cheek, just like she was kissing me, then nuzzled my carrot pocket.

After feeding her a few choice pieces, I haltered her and swung up on her back. The usual undignified flailing across her back ensued, and then finally my leg kicked over her thin side, and I was safely astraddle. Good thing Mick with the camera was long gone. I would hate to have that moment captured on film.

As she walked peacefully towards the barn, I leaned across her neck, stretching my arms around her.

"Gidget, how can we help that poor Sheridan?"

She flicked her ears back at me, and tossed her head in Milly's direction. Milly was busily saddling the three trail horses.

I wondered if Milly could help. Milly certainly had compassion for horses, and was always full of common sense advice. But how could I ask Milly without divulging my traitorous intention to work at Heritage? I couldn't. I hated that this secret was growing anchors that were dragging down my good intentions.

In the barn, I quickly exchanged Gidget's halter for her hackamore, and led her out to the trail group. The threesome had already gathered and Milly was helping them mount. She introduced me to the man, woman, and teenage boy.

The boy wore dorky glasses, and had an overgrown crop of acne. I was glad I was the trail guide rather than Mick. I may have noticed the boy had some glaring complexion issues, but I was compassionate enough to keep those thoughts to myself. If it had been Mick leading the trail, he would have been compelled to say things like, "So Four-eyes, apparently your vision isn't corrected enough to find the Clearasil aisle at the drug store?"

Usually he didn't spout such taunts to the poor victim's face, but he always found a way to insult in some underhanded way. I should know. I'd been the target enough times to qualify as an expert on the matter.

Instead of spewing insults, I just smiled at my little group, and nudged Gidget towards the trail head. Gidget swished her long, silky, grey tail. Her hooves clattered across the gravel driveway as she stepped pertly, her ears perked eagerly forward. She was totally embracing her new role.

"You ride without a saddle?" the dorky young man said.

I never understood those kinds of questions. What if I said *No?* Would the logical inconsistency fry his brain? I was tempted to respond the way Mick always did to questions like that. *Oh no! I wonder how it fell off without me even noticing?* Instead, I turned, leaning my hand on Gidget's rump and said, "I ride every day. You get used to it. How about you? Is this your first time on a horse?"

This was definitely a good guess since he was clutching the saddle horn with both hands, and the reins lay untouched across his horse's withers.

"I rode at Heritage Farm once," he said. "Those horses are a little peppier than these ones and I was a little nervous."

His knuckles were drained of all color, squeezing the saddle horn with all his might.

"You don't need to be nervous with these horses. They are really calm. Almost comatose most of the time."

He laughed. He had nice teeth. Very straight. I felt oddly happy for him over that, in the midst of his less than stellar complexion. I appreciated that he'd laughed at my joke, lame as it was. Also, my ears perked up immediately at the mention of Heritage Farm.

"What did you think of Heritage Farm?" I asked.

Gidget's ears flicked back and forth as we plodded along. She seemed to be interested in the discussion.

"Honestly, I would never go back there."

"Really? Why not?"

"It's really pretty, and the trail horses are a little bit nicer than these ones...sorry..."

"It's ok. Most are."

"But when we started off on the trail, I saw someone leading out a really nice looking dark horse. The horse tried to lie down, like it was in pain or something. The guy started hitting it with his whip right in the face."

It had to be Sheridan.

"When was this?"

"I don't know. Maybe a month ago. The horse squealed, and it looked like he tried to get up, but then he just rolled back onto his side. The man started whipping him all over till he finally managed to get up. I felt so sorry for the horse."

"We would have reported it," the mother said, "But we didn't know who to talk to. We did tell the owners we would not be back because of that. They assured us the horse had issues with balking and the trainer knew what he was doing."

"That's just cruel," the boy said. His face contorted as though he were about to cry. Then he sneezed like a firecracker was lodged in his nose.

Gidget suddenly leaped sideways as a girl popped out of the underbrush at the same moment as the explosive sneeze. I hung on to her mane, and gathered the reins. "Ho, girl, ho!" She pranced and sidestepped, but didn't bolt as I'd feared she would. If that had happened even six months ago, I'd likely be hanging by my ponytail from a low hanging branch and Gidget would be half way to Toledo. One of us was getting better.

Fiora! And she had materialized at the same spot where she'd emerged a few days ago when Mick was leading the trail. Was she waiting here for him?

"I wanted to talk to you," she said, her gravelly voice causing Gidget to shake her head. Gidget was a good judge of character.

"Me?" I said, "Why? You can walk alongside if you must, but I need to lead this trail."

She glanced back at the boy, who was ogling her with the same stupefied look Mick always had in her presence. "Dream on," she said to him, then turned back to me.

"I hear you will be teaching at Heritage."

I shot a look at the boy behind me. She spoke quietly. I hoped he could not hear.

"No, I haven't decided."

"There's some bad stuff going on there," she said.

We had reached the section where we did our short uphill trot. I was totally intrigued, but had no choice but to cut her off.

"I can't talk now," I said. "But what bad stuff?"

"Watch that horse Sheridan. Someone has to help him, and I can't."

I couldn't believe my ears. This harlot, this little vamp with the clothes that wouldn't fit a Barbie doll had a heart? I don't know what she thought I could do, if she knew she couldn't help him.

"I will help you, but I can't go near the farm. They banned me. Can I meet you after your trail ride?" she asked.

I shook my head. She made my skin crawl but her concern for Sheridan seemed genuine. "Why didn't you ask Mick?" I whispered.

"He can't do anything. They will hurt his father if he tries to expose what they are doing. They have hurt others. I have an idea but I need your help. Can you meet me back here?"

"I can't," I said, "I have to help with the chores and then get home."

She nodded, saying, "Figures," and melted back into the underbrush. Frankly she gave me chills. Nonetheless, I almost wished I'd agreed to meet her.

"That was weird," said the boy, "What did she want?"

Good. He hadn't heard.

"Directions," I called back. "Ok, everyone. This is the fun part. We trot up this hill. Just kick your horses' sides, and hang on to the saddle horn. It's bumpier than a walk but we won't go far."

"Trot!" I said to Gidget, who leaped forward. I got the sense that she was a little creeped out by Fiora's strange presence as well, and wanted to get out of there. I know I sure did.

Chapter Five

Mick and Burton returned right before the evening feeding time. I raced over to Mick, and pulled him aside.

"What happened? Did you see Sheridan?"

He patted his pocket, where the camera bulged.

"Got a picture."

"Of what?"

"Mr. Bank's daughter. Man, she was almost as cute as Bella."

"Mick! Seriously?"

"Yes, pin-head, but that's not all. I also got a picture of the wraps on Sheridan's pastern, and the chains. None of that is illegal though."

"What about inside his shoes?"

"Dad didn't shoe him. I think they talked about him, and Dad's going back. They went off to the side to talk. I didn't hear much of it. I think their farrier just quit and they're desperate. I missed most of what they talked about though."

Now that was not at all like Mick. His stealth skills were legendary. If he wanted to, he could sneak past the Secret Service.

"I had to be pretty clever to get near Sheridan. That trainer is awfully suspicious. So I interrogated the daughter while Dad was talking with Mr. Banks." He grinned, lifting his eyebrows, with a suggestive leer.

That was why he hadn't overheard Burton's private talk with Mr. Banks. He'd been distracted by the daughter.

"Dad's going back in a couple of days, so I'm guessing Sheridan is on the list to be shod."

I filed that information away. I wondered what the private discussion had been about. If it was above board, wouldn't Mr. Banks have said it in front of Mick? Was Burton agreeing to shoe Sheridan in a way that contributed to soring? I'd read that lots of farriers and even vets were in collusion with the trainers. Would Burton do that?

"Mick!" Burton called, "Hay time!"

I followed Mick into the barn. He scampered into the hay loft, tossing bales out the side window for the field horses, and a few bales on the main barn floor for the indoor horses.

This was one of my favorite times at the farm. The animals all knew it was chow time, and gathered in clumps near the feed bins. The cows mooed, the horses nickered, the chickens clucked, and the goats bleated. I loved the chorus of animals as the sun yawned in the waning day, and long, dark shadows stretched across the hard packed dirt.

Milly and Peeper, bookends with long braids down their backs, both lugged heavy pails of grain to the goats. The bleating dropped to silence as the greedy goats pounced on the grain. The pigtailed pair moved on to the grunting pigs next. As the slop filled the feed bins, the pigs snuffled with staccato guttural sounds.

The endless waves of barn cats mewed, weaving their bodies under the goats' legs as Milly milked. Peeper tied her own goat to the fence and joined her mother, the swish-swish of the milk spurting to the inside of the pail.

I stood watching them, transfixed, lulled by the sounds of the animals.

"Earth to cranium-minimus!" Mick called.

I swung around.

"Where do you go…when you go there?" he asked.

I shrugged, and followed him to load the bales onto the flatbed.

"Here's a clue for your mystery," Mick said, "No horse steps with *'big licks'* unless something evil is done to him."

"What is *big lick?*"

"That goofy high step that looks like they have puppet strings attached to their hooves. All the evidence you need is in the way Sheridan walks. You don't need a picture of nails in his shoes gouging his flesh…though they are probably there."

"Then why isn't it stopped if it is so obvious?"

"No one cares," Mick said. "People like watching the horses with *big lick* strides. What's a little torture in exchange for all that excitement?"

Soon the flatbed was covered with the bales, and Milly, who had finished milking, opened the gate to the pasture. Burton fired up the old tractor and drove it through the wide gate. Mick and I both sprinted after the rumbling tractor, and hopped onto the back of the flatbed.

As it bounced across the field, I swung my legs and wondered about people who dismissed cruelty to a horse. Gidget stood in the distance, near Trinity, watching the tractor totter across the rutted pasture. When the rest of the herd began trotting towards the round metal feed bin, she perked her ears, and nudged Trinity. The two of them swung their heads and trotted at the rear of the hungry herd.

"If I were you," Mick said, "I'd take the job teaching the horse-ercise class. Then you can put on your teensy weensy thinking cap and see if you can find evidence of soring with Sheridan."

I gazed at him. Did he actually care? Was there a desire for humane treatment of any creature other than himself in his conscience? It almost seemed that way.

"Who would I report it to, if I found it?" I asked.

"I don't know. *You're* the Einstein in this friendship."

Friendship?

"Speaking of friends, your buddy Fiora stopped me on the trail ride today."

That got his interest.

"What did she want with you? Probably not to make a wig out of your hair, I bet."

"Very funny. No. She wants to help Sheridan."

His mouth fell open and he turned to stare at me. "Now *that's* very funny."

"It surprised me too, but she wasn't kidding. I think it actually bothers her."

Mick scratched his forehead looking puzzled.

"Maybe there's more to her than meets the eye," I said, "Though not much more." There just wasn't much *left* to meet the eye since her clothes concealed less than 1% *at most* of her body.

Mick actually laughed at that. "Well her dad *is* a trainer of Tennessee Walking Horses. She probably knows first-hand what kind of clever torment is devised for Sheridan."

Now it was my turn for my jaw to drop open.

"Does he do soring?" I wasn't sure if that was the right terminology. Fortunately, Mick had no experience in the world of these expensive show horses, so he didn't know much more than I did. Otherwise, he would not have been shy pointing out my errors.

"I imagine. Most of the *big lick* horses are sored…and her dad works with some big names."

Well. No wonder Fiora couldn't expose the abuse of Sheridan. I had read that the horse industry turned a blind eye to soring. There was a code of silence to protect the livelihood of the owners, trainers, farriers, and vets that worked with the Tennessee Walking Horses. Everyone involved in soring knew that to implicate one meant danger to all of them. What would I do if my dad was involved in something so despicable? Maybe I would dress like a street-walker too.

Later, when I told Bella, she hugged me. "It sounds like you are learning to be merciful towards Fiora."

"I wouldn't go that far," I warned her.

"Don't be ashamed of it. Mercy is a great characteristic. If God didn't show us mercy for all the terrible things we do, we would all be doomed."

"She did surprise me," I said. "She doesn't *look* like someone who would care about a horse."

"The way you described how the trainer dressed, he sounded pretty respectable. I guess you can't always tell by the outfit what's inside."

"Or lack of outfit, in Fiora's case."

"So what will you do?" she asked.

"I'll go Sunday, and then decide."

I went to the library the following morning. Miss Scruggs, who hadn't seen me since my tearful collapse when I first read about soring, came rushing over when I entered her little sanctuary.

"How are you, dear?" she asked.

"I'm good, Miss Scruggs. I need some help. Who would I report horse abuse to if I saw it?"

"Does this have to do with what you read last week that so upset you?"

I nodded.

Miss Scruggs asked me some more questions about the specific abuse and then found the new law that made it illegal to show or transport a horse who was the victim of soring.

Listen to what we found! It was repulsive. The Animal Protection Act of 1970 prohibited sored horses from participating in shows, exhibitions, sales or auctions. It also prohibited drivers from transporting sored horses to or from any of these events. I read the act several times with Miss Scruggs. I was only 14-years-old and even I saw the glaring omission. Soring *itself* was not illegal. Only showing and transporting sored horses was punishable.

I lost a lot of faith that afternoon in our legal system. Why would laws be written that would prohibit the sored horses to show, but would not prohibit the inhumane cruelty itself? I was stuck. It didn't matter if I could prove that Sheridan was a victim of soring. I could do *nothing* unless (until) he entered a show.

Miss Scruggs told me that even if the act didn't specifically outlaw soring, it might still help for me to report a trainer who I knew was using those terrible techniques. Then they could catch him at a show. She discovered that the responsible department was a sub-department of the USDA called the Animal and Plant Health Inspection Service. She patted my back and promised me she would help me find out everything I needed to call them when I had evidence of soring.

"How do I get proof?" I asked, laying my head on the stack of books we'd perused for information.

"You have your farrier friend," she said. "Talk to him. You have a camera. Take pictures of the horse's feet, and when the trainer whips him. Get pictures of the horse lying down, and being forced to stand. Each one may not be enough alone, but together, they might be."

I thanked her. It felt impossible. I was 14-years-old. This practice of soring had been going on for decades. If the horse industry itself wouldn't stop it…how could I? How was one (small-headed) little girl to stop such a pervasive practice?

Bella listened to me moan and complain for a half hour that night over the phone.

"You don't have to stop *all* soring," she said, "Maybe all you have to do now is stop one."

"How?"

"I can tell you a Bible story that might help."

Of course she could. "Have at it," I told her.

"Have you ever heard of Esther?"

"No."

"Esther was an orphan, adopted by her uncle during the time of the Persian King Xerxes. At that time, the Jews were in captivity, and under the rule of Persia. Esther herself was a Jew. King Xerxes wanted a new wife after his queen ticked him off. I won't go into all that, but honestly, if I'd been queen, I would have done the same thing."

"This sounds juicy."

"It is. So the king holds a kingdom-wide contest for the best candidate to be the new queen. Mordecai, Esther's uncle, tells her to enter the contest. She does, and wins. She's the new Queen. Now Xerxes doesn't know she is a Jew. A really terrible guy named Haman wants to kill all the Jews and manages to trick the king into issuing a decree to allow him to do just that. There's a whole bunch of back story, but you can read it yourself. I'm summarizing."

I leaned forward, captivated. "You are doing a great job too. This is in the Bible? It sounds like an R-rated movie."

"The Bible is way racier than you would think. I mean it is the history of real people, after all. Anyway, Mordecai hears about Haman's plot and runs to tell Queen Esther. He tells her she must go to the king, tell him she's a Jew, and beg for the deliverance of her people. She is terrified to do so because there was a rule that she could not approach the king unless he summoned her. She could be killed if she disobeyed that rule."

"That's harsh."

"Persia was a rough culture back then."

"So what happened? Did she go to the king?"

"Well, she whined and said *I am just one person, what can I do....*" Here Bella paused. She was clearly insuring I caught her drift, which I did since she was about as subtle as a heart attack.

"And Mordecai tells her: *if you remain silent at this time, relief and deliverance for the Jews will arise from another place, but you and your father's family will perish. And who knows but that you have come to your royal position for such a time as this?*"

"Wow."

"Yeah. Powerful stuff."

"Does she go to the king?"

"She does, and in the end, the Jews are saved because of her courage."

I held the phone to my ear, without speaking.

"Are you still there?" Bella asked.

"I'm not in a royal position," I answered, finally.

"No analogy is ever perfect," Bella said.

Chapter Six

You can not imagine my dismay when Sunday morning I showed up at Heritage Farm, and guess who else was there? Burton. He stared at me with confusion at first, and then anger. Mick was not with him this time.

When Mr. Banks ducked out to the pasture for the horse Burton would first be working on, Burton confronted me.

"What the ##$#@*&* are you doing here?"

He didn't normally cuss around me, or at least *at* me, so I knew he was really mad. I didn't have much time to fill him in. Mr. Banks was already entering the back of the barn with the horse for Burton to shoe.

"I am helping with a class they want to start, but only on Sundays. It won't affect my work with you at all."

Burton shifted his attention to the horse Mr. Banks was snapping to cross ties.

"Anything you need, just holler," Mr. Banks said, "Vicky and I will be looking over some horses she will be helping us with in some volunteer work."

Burton nodded gruffly, and didn't look at me. I could tell he was boiling, and probably figured out what volunteer work Mr. Banks was talking about. I felt like a heel, but what was done was done.

Mr. Banks brought me out to the pasture to meet the "farm matrons" as he called them. They were probably not as old as Burton's horses, but they did not look like the show horses I'd seen in the barn either.

As I met each horse, Mr. Banks asked lots of questions. How many kids in a class? How did Milly advertise to get students? How long was each class and each session? I evaded some questions, like how she advertised. That really didn't seem like his business.

Then, he told me we could go in the barn, and he would give me paper to write down what a typical class would look like with some specific exercises. I was feeling guiltier and guiltier by the moment. Still, I sat at the end of the barn with the pad he gave me, and drew pictures of some of the exercises.

He was impressed. He hadn't known I was an artist. He said the pictures would be very useful in implementing the class. Some of my unease melted with how nice he was to me. He was also really nice to the "farm matrons." How could he turn a blind eye to the abuse of Sheridan while treating the old mares so kindly?

Burton glanced up from his work now and then, watching me for a moment with disdain. Would he ban me from his farm? I would die if he did that.

Mr. Banks told me that he wanted me to use his youngest daughter, Jessy, as a demonstration, and show him what I did with the kids during the class. His youngest daughter was just a little older than Peeper. She was much more polite than Peeper. Not a single cuss word spewed out of her the way it did out of Peeper, as though from a salt shaker with too many holes.

Then Burton told him the horse he was working on was done. Who was next? Mr. Banks gave me a quick look, and waited till I started off with his daughter. As I headed down the aisle, I saw Sheridan's trainer walk in and I knew who was next.

You'd be amazed at my craftiness. I sent little Jessy to go catch the mare we would use for the demonstration. Then I stood just outside the back barn door, with my ear against the crack. I could see the trainer enter Sheridan's stall, and I heard groaning. I deduced that Sheridan was lying down again, and from the sounds of a snapping whip, the trainer was forcing him up.

The shouts grew angrier, and from what I could tell, Sheridan was still refusing. I was just about to rush in when I heard Burton's voice.

"That horse is in pain."

"We think he has issues with the left shoe," Mr. Banks said. "We'd like you to reshoe him."

"Not without a vet to look at him," Burton said.

"He shows next weekend," the trainer added. "We pay top dollar if you can help us get him ready. Our vet has been treating him."

I didn't hear clearly what was said next, but I could tell they had gotten Sheridan to his feet. When I heard their voices fade as they rounded the corner into the main room of the barn, I snuck back in and tiptoed to the edge of the aisle. I peeked very slowly around the corner. Sheridan was in the cross ties. Burton was already pulling off one of the old shoes.

"This horse has an abscess in the sole," Burton said. "And from the looks and smell, has had it for some time."

"Just pad it and put the shoe back on," the trainer ordered.

"No." Burton stood up. "This horse can barely walk. He has laminitis at best and likely foundering. He needs a vet immediately."

"All we need is for him to make it to the show next week," the trainer said.

"This horse will not be able to walk at all by next week," Burton said. "I'm not certain he can be healed at all with how badly that laminae is infected and inflamed already."

There was some hushed discussion between Mr. Banks and the trainer. I think I heard the word, "euthanized," from Burton, and "slaughter auction" from Mr. Banks. There were some more whispered outbursts from the trainer, and then I heard Burton say he'd play no part in helping this animal suffer.

"I will report you," he said, "Unless you have this horse euthanized now."

"You pay the slaughter fee, and you can take the horse," said Mr. Banks. "You understand that we request the condition of the horse be kept quiet. It might hurt your business with other farms if they knew their practices were criticized by a farrier."

Burton swore, and said he was not paying them any money for a horse that should be humanely put down. "You know you can't take this horse to auction with these scars and in this condition. Besides the fact that to help this horse will cost a bundle and I don't even know if he can be saved."

It was at this point in the discussion that I did a very stupid, and impulsive thing. I had $300 saved from my work for Burton's Farm and from Dr. Creola. I had hoped it would eventually be enough to buy Gidget. However, Gidget would have to wait.

I sprinted around the corner and said, "Is $300 enough?"

The three men looked at me with varying degrees of horror and anger. I understood instantly why they had hired a kid to run the class. A kid would not dare challenge what they were doing, or know how to report it. They would try to bolster the farm's reputation with my class, and figured I posed little danger of reporting or understanding what they were doing to Sheridan. I don't know how I knew that, but I was certain of it. It all made sense now. I crumpled the class notes I'd drawn into my pocket.

"We won't report it," Burton growled, "If you let us take the horse now. And we are not paying you a cent."

"That would be satisfactory," Mr. Banks said.

Burton told me to run to the farm, and tell Mick to drive the trailer over. He also told me to have Milly call Dr. Creola and have him meet us at the barn.

I was already racing out of the barn, and heard Burton asking for rags and tape. He would not put the shoes back on, but needed to wrap the hooves enough to protect poor Sheridan and cushion the hoof. I was ecstatic and ready to run all the way to Burton's farm to get Matt. But first, I paused, looked straight into Mr. Bank's eyes, and smiled. "By the way, I quit."

Milly didn't even ask me what I had been doing at Heritage Farm. She listened to my story. Heaving a troubled sigh, she said, "I'll call Dr. Creola. What does Burton think we plan to pay with?"

"I have money," I blurted. "I told Burton I would pay. Will it be more than $300?" She touched my cheek briefly, batting moist eyes, and then turned to go call Dr. Creola. I didn't feel guilty about having gone to Heritage anymore since I knew Bella was right. I was *supposed* to be there, royal position or not, for such a time as this. Just like Bella said.

Meanwhile, Mick was thrilled to hitch the trailer to the truck. He had just gotten his license and had never driven the truck with the trailer before. It was only a mile, but I wondered if Burton was too trusting. Mick almost jack-knifed the trailer backing up. Metal crunched, and he burned some rubber jerking forward. I hopped in the truck beside him.

"What are you doing, hay-head?"

"Taking my life in my hands, it looks like."

He sighed and roared out of the driveway, slamming me against my door. The empty old trailer rattled behind us.

As we started down the highway, I cast a look at the pasture. Gidget stood near the fence, watching us. My heart dropped. Not that there had ever been a huge chance of me buying her, but now that possibility was certainly gone. It had taken me my entire life to earn that $300. I had to do it though. There had been no choice.

When we reached Heritage Farm, Burton was already gathering his tools. The hoof was wrapped with rags. Poor Sheridan. Despite the obvious pain he was in, he hobbled behind Burton. Mick opened the rusty back door of the trailer, and it swung on creaking hinges.

Neither Mr. Banks nor the trainer were anywhere in sight.

Burton paused with Sheridan.

"Get my tools, Mick," he said. I reached out and stroked Sheridan's neck. He looked into my eyes. Burton clucked, and led him into the trailer.

"You drive my truck," Burton said to Mick, "I'll drive the trailer home."

I hopped into the truck with Burton. He was surprised. I had to clear the air.

"Burton, I'm sorry about the class. I didn't think it would hurt your farm but now I know it was not a good idea."

He nodded.

"And I meant what I said. I have $300 saved and I will pay for Dr. Creola to help Sheridan. And I will teach your horse-ercise classes for free if that isn't enough."

Burton nodded again. I think it was insulting that he had to accept help from a kid, but he had no choice. I knew that. He would not have taken Sheridan otherwise. Being poor *stunk*.

"What will you do with your horse if he survives?"

"*My* horse?"

"You bought him."

Well. I guess I did. I owned a horse. A horse that might not live, and if he did might be permanently lame and never able to be ridden. And come to think about it…if it was my horse, how would I pay the board?

"I'll make a deal with you," Burton said, "You cover his vet bills and his hay. If he recovers, we'll talk about what we do after that."

I turned around and looked through the trailer window at my horse. *My* horse!

Dr. Creola arrived shortly after we backed Sheridan out of the trailer. The poor horse lay down almost instantly.

I kneeled by his head and stroked his forehead. He looked at me, grunting softly. I waved flies away, those dastardly ever-present flies. It occurred to me again that God must have been only half-awake when He made flies. There just was no other explanation, other than the probability that God was fiction.

Sheridan barely moved as Dr. Creola carefully helped Burton remove the rags around his hooves.

"Well," Dr. Creola said, "Both feet have laminitis. The left is worse, with that abscess. You are right Burton, though anyone with a nose can tell it is infected. This poor horse is in a lot of pain."

"Can he be healed?" I asked.

Dr. Creola didn't answer immediately. I continued stroking Sheridan's neck and shoeing away the nasty flies.

"He seems awfully docile and amenable considering how much he must hurt," Burton said. "He never put up a fight at all while I was removing the shoes. It has to have been painful."

"Sored horses are trained not to react to the pain," I said.

Burton and Dr.Creola stared at me. Mick chuckled, looking at me with a tinge of admiration. Maybe it was disdain. Hard to tell with Mick. "You would never suspect such a little head could be so smart."

"How did you know that?" Dr. Creola asked me.

"I researched it."

"To help Sheridan?"

"Yes."

Dr. Creola examined the left hoof again. A fly landed on my arm and bit me. "Ouch! I hate these flies!" I cried, smacking it away.

Dr. Creola looked up slowly. "Flies… you know, with a horse in this much discomfort, draining and cleaning that abscess is going to be unbearable. But there is an alternative. Maggots."

"Maggots!" I said. "As in baby flies??"

"That's gross," Mick said.

"It may be gross," Dr. Creola agreed, "But it is one of the safest, most effective, and least painful ways to debride an infected wound like this. It might be worth a shot. The other treatments won't cost much either, but they will take time and effort."

He looked at me. "Are you willing to go find the maggots? And then put in the hours of attention Sheridan will need with the other therapies as he heals?"

I hesitated a moment. *Where does one get maggots? Should I ask?* "Yes."

"Do you want to know what you will need to do before you commit?" he asked.

"Okay."

"First, he will need a box stall big enough to comfortably lay down. I am willing to give him Trinity's for now. The weather is beautiful and she enjoys being out with the other horses. Then you need to line the bottom of the stall with several inches of wood shavings, and then another deep layer of straw. He will need baggies of ice around his front hooves every hour during the day, at least till the inflammation calms down. 20 minutes on each hour. Can you do that?"

I nodded.

"He'll need antibiotics and the maggot dressing changed regularly, but I will do that. Oh, and Milly, keep high sugar feed at a minimum. I'd recommend Timothy hay."

Milly grimaced. I guess it was either expensive or hard to get a hold of.

"If that is not possible," he said, "You can soak your regular hay in warm water for thirty minutes before feeding. That leeches excess sugar from it."

"I can do that. What's wrong with sugar?" I asked.

"Sugar results in high blood insulin, and contributes to laminitis. These show horses are often fed a very sugar rich diet, the worse thing possible for their laminae health. Also, he'll need some high protein food like soybean to help with the hoof growth and repair."

Milly nodded. She mixed soybeans already with the grain.

"How often do I need to get the maggots?"

"I can help with the maggots," Mick said, "I love maggots."

I didn't know whether to be grateful, or disgusted.

"The first batch of maggots may be all we need. If the maggots get fat from having lots of infected goo to eat, they need to be changed every two or three days. When they stay skinny, and die, we know the wound is clean. Their saliva is soothing, so the horse will feel better once they start doing their magic."

"This is going to be fun," Mick said, enjoying the contortions in my greenish face.

"It's not going to be easy," Dr. Creola said, "But he seems like a sweet horse, and he might pull through. With lots of work and prayer."

I will pray, I thought. If God managed to come up with such an unexpected good reason for the flies I so detested, maybe He was worth talking to. It certainly couldn't hurt.

Chapter Seven

I will not relate where we found the maggots or how we harvested them. There is only so much churning of the gut one can take. I was honestly beholden to Mick because I could not have done what was necessary. Not even to save a horse.

I also will not describe what they looked like when Dr. Creola dumped them in Sheridan's oozing hoof, before repacking and taping with the soft towels. Sheridan heaved a deep sigh, however, as though in relief. Whatever magic was in the maggot saliva, Sheridan appreciated it.

The priciest part of Dr. Creola's treatment, which he said was unavoidable, was x-raying Sheridan's hooves. That transpired while Mick and I were out harvesting maggots. Dr. Creola said the biggest danger with laminitis was that it would pull the major toe bone out of position. When it did that, it became the more serious problem called founder, and there was less chance a horse could be helped. Dr. Creola reported that Sheridan's bones were still aligned properly, and that was a very good thing. Miraculous, in fact.

Besides being on maggot duty, I was in charge of icing Sheridan's hooves. I decided the best way to accomplish that was by devising icepacks I could tie on his legs. Not to sound conceited, but I really do believe my hoof icepacks were exceptionally clever. Even Mick complimented me on those.

I ripped up an old raincoat. (Well, to be truthful, it wasn't old *until* I ripped it, but felt there was no need to tell Mom that.) Then I sewed three of the four sides of the rubber rectangles, leaving one side open. I sewed lace ties at the top of the rubber ice bags. All I had to do was fill the bags with ice, and then I tied them around Sheridan's hooves. He was a prince, always standing quietly while I worked around his sore feet.

Since I didn't have to hold the ice bags on, I had twenty minutes to dash out and work with Gidget and Trinity every hour. In between icing sessions, I did the farm chores.

Gidget was always eager to see me. I could tell she missed me. Nonetheless, she always waited patiently, often gazing at the barn with an expectant look on her face. I had to forego trail guiding since the icing was every hour. Dr. Creola said that would only be necessary the first couple of weeks.

I told Gidget that the wait would be worth it. She would have a new friend. She nibbled at my cheek. A horse kiss. She'd just started doing that. I think it was her way of showing me she understood.

Mick took over most of the training of Trinity, but told me he wouldn't charge me. He said he would contribute his share that he certainly deserved to the Save-Sheridan fund. I was grateful, but sorry that I was missing out on the summer of riding, again! Last summer it was my broken tail bone, and this summer, my broken horse. Life sure never went the way I planned.

At first, Sheridan spent most of the days lying down. The first week, we had to find a new batch of maggots every three days. Despite being the best friend known to man, Bella refused to help with the maggot hunt. She told me she loved me and would do almost anything to help me, but not this.

"I'm pretty impressed *you* are willing to do this," said Mick, as I held open a sack into which he shoveled the maggots. I held back a gag, turning my head and nose as far as possible from the carcass that hosted the maggots. "Not every girl would be willing to do this. Is it because you feel a kinship to the maggots?"

"I would do it." A seductive voice gurgled out of the dark coolness of the forest. Fiora. I hadn't seen her since the day she'd asked me to help Sheridan so long ago. She stepped out of the shadows into a patch of light. She was just as barely dressed as always. I wondered if she wore more layers in the winter.

Mick almost dropped the wriggling mass of maggots. In a dream-like state, he plopped them into the bag. I quickly tied a string around it to insure it remained as tightly closed as humanly possible.

"Thank you for helping that horse," Fiora said, "though they will just find another."

"They wouldn't give us Sheridan if we reported them," I said.

"I thought you were a clever girl," Fiora purred.

Frankly, I don't know where she would have gotten that idea. And the comment stung. I had felt awful knowing we had done nothing to stop what that evil trainer was doing to other horses. Bella and I spent hours talking about how we could keep him from harming other horses, but came up empty.

"Not that clever," I said. Mick didn't say a word. He still looked at Fiora as though he'd been drugged.

"Well, bye. Thanks for your help Mick." I held the slightly writhing sack at arms' length and headed back to Burton's Farm. I knew Mick would not be joining me.

Gidget saw me as I cut across the pasture. She whinnied and loped along the fence till she reached me. She stopped a little distance away, snorting at the sight (and smell) of the maggot bag. Her shying instincts were not entirely erased, though in this case, I didn't blame her. Who wouldn't recoil from that? She'd waited all day to see me. Now, getting a whiff of the maggots and carcass remains, she decided she could wait a little longer.

Chapter Eight

Poor Sheridan barely stood up at all for the first few days. Dr. Creola watched Burton rewrap the towels and tape them in place around his hooves. I was nearby watching, though truth be told, I closed my eyes during the changing of the maggots.

"I wish we could cushion his soles more," Dr. Creola said, "The maggots are really fat, so they are doing a good job eating up the dead tissue. I like how the abscess looks. I just wish we could make Sheridan more comfortable."

"Isn't there some stuff you could stick in there to numb his feet?" I said. I knew there was because I knew the nasty 'soring' trainers used it to fool any inspectors who might examine their horses before a show. It would numb the feet long enough for the horses to remain unperturbed during the examination of poking and prodding, but short-lasting so their sole would be sore when they went in the ring. It was the sore hooves that made the horse pull his legs up so quickly and so high.

"There is, but I don't want to use it," Dr. Creola answered. Bella was with me, and she also had averted her eyes during the maggot exchange. In fact, she had run to the far end of the barn, and peeked around the corner until I told her all was clear, maggots safely wrapped inside the hoof.

"Why don't you want to use it?" she asked, creeping back to Sheridan's stall.

"Pain is what prevents him from standing on those inflamed soles and causing more damage. If I numb him, it could actually make him worse."

As Bella and I walked home that night, she told me, "I was thinking about what Dr. Creola said about pain."

I'd been thinking about that too. I had no idea how to cushion Sheridan's feet so he could stand safely without pain, but I was flopping it around in every direction in my head.

"God uses pain too."

I looked at Bella. Her voice broke. She was not at all a pessimist, and always filled with joy. The sadness in her tone was not usual.

"When Mom died, I would have loved something to numb me from how empty I felt. Not only for how much I hurt, but for how much Maria hurt. There was no way to help Maria understand why Mom was gone."

I nodded. I would have given anything to have the slightest bit of comforting words to share, but as usual, came up empty. I tried to plaster compassion across by face, in lieu of wise, healing words.

"I asked God to take away the pain. But that didn't happen. Not for a long time. I wondered why God would allow me, and especially Maria, to suffer so strongly. He could have removed the pain if He wanted to."

I failed to see the parallel with Sheridan's plight. Yes, in Sheridan's case the pain was necessary or he would walk on his fragile hooves. What purpose did the pain of a dead mother bring?

"I still don't know God's plan in all that, except it brought us home from China. There was definite benefit in that, which we couldn't see then so easily. But why all the pain?" She paused, absently twirling a piece of her hair in her fingers as she considered that unanswerable quandary. "It's true, I learned some things."

"Like what?" I asked. This was not purely academic to me. I had suffered terribly when my old horse Joe died. I still saw no redeeming benefit from that. Frankly, I was not thrilled with God over that incident, if indeed God was there.

"I learned I could endure pain." She smiled weakly.

"If He just took pain away, you wouldn't need that lesson," I said.

"Yes. So there must be a purpose to pain. In Sheridan's case, Dr. Creola explained what that was. It will ultimately help him heal. In the Bible, there's a verse in Hosea about pain. *Come, let us return to the Lord; for he has torn us, that he may heal us; he has struck us down, and he will bind us up."*

I waited. This was not clearing up my confusion. In fact, it made it worse. God *himself* ripped us apart so He could heal us? I doubt this was Bella's intent, but that verse was totally turning me off to God. In fact, it sounded similar to Mick's twisted logic.

"According to that verse, pain must be how God helps us recognize our need for Him." Bella was a whole lot more eager to give the benefit of the doubt than I was.

"Didn't you know that already, before your Mom died?" I asked.

"I thought I did," she said, "But I didn't know how much till my mom died. It shook my world. I mean, if something as important as a mother wasn't guaranteed, then nothing was secure."

God, if He was a god with any kind of clout, could surely *make* it secure. He chose not to. I still didn't think Bella was making a convincing case for the wonderful invention of pain or for the concept of God as anything but a sadistic beast. I kept my mouth shut however. I knew enough about pain as not to add to it.

"At first, I just felt grief, and unbearable pain, and then fear. But then I thought about what was secure in life and there was one thing. That gave me some peace."

"What one thing?" I wracked my brain trying to figure out what that could be. It definitely wasn't Strawberry Cheesecake, because I'd been promised a piece would be saved for me when I was home late from the farm Sunday and one of my greedy siblings ate it.

"God Himself. He is always there."

That sounded like He was a bully to me. Knock everything out of your hand just so you will hold His. Again, I felt it was best not to share my thoughts since Bella seemed ok with the concept.

"And it made me more sensitive to others who were struggling without a mother. I would rather have had my own mom live, but at least I can help others. In fact, I wonder about Fiora. She seems like someone who doesn't have a mother's guidance to me."

Bella was *way* more noble than I would have been. I didn't agree with her at all that this gave God a pass on the whole pain deal, but I did admire her. However, I could not agree, nor even understand, her blasted insistence of giving Fiora the benefit of the doubt.

"Dad always says God's purpose is not to pamper us, but to perfect us. Pain is one way He accomplishes that."

Suddenly, I thought of a solution. I knew what I could do to help cushion Sheridan's feet! It came in a flash with Bella's last statement.

"Thanks for listening to me," Bella said, "I don't know where all that came from. It just popped in my head. You are such a good listener."

We had reached her house, and I was already trotting towards home. I barely even waved, so filled with the vision of how I could help Sheridan.

"You helped me a lot!" I said.

When I got home, I raced to my little sister's closet. I remembered we had a stash of disposable diapers left over from when she was potty trained. Mom said Pampers were the single best invention of the 20th century.

I used duct tape and fashioned a hoof-shaped form with the Pampers. *God's* purpose may not be to *pamper* us, but mine was! I could barely stand waiting till the next day dawned. I gathered my bag of duct tape and hoof mold of Pampers and dashed out right after breakfast.

Early summer mornings in Chazak were just as wonderful as the dusk with its fireflies and cool breezes. The sun was just awakening and stretching its long golden arms against the sky. Robins were already poking around in the grass, listening for worms. The normally noisy Narroway highway was silent. A stray car chugged past now and then as I jogged along the road, but mostly the only sounds were birds chirping in the trees.

I was so glad Burton had already arrived. The summer was busy at the farm with the trail rides, and his increased farrier work. He was often there before the rest of his family. He was feeding Marmaduke and the stallion when I trotted into the yard.

He waved, and asked what I had in the bag.

"I had an idea for Sheridan," I said. I pulled out the Pamper Hoof shield. Burton cocked his head, and squinted.

"Diapers?"

"It's to go around his hoof," I said, "To cushion his sole so maybe he can walk a little more easily."

Burton's eyes widened, and his face broke into a grin as he reached out for my invention.

"That's clever. It is thicker and more spongy than the towel wrap. It would stay dryer too."

"Will it work?" I asked.

"It might. Let's go see Sheridan."

Sheridan was lying down in his stall, as usual. He nickered when he saw me. I always greeted him with a carrot, and he knew I would be the one to ice his hooves. I think the icing gave him at least momentary relief. His eyes lost their tinge of anguish when I iced the hooves.

Burton left the towels wrapped around his hooves, and with my help, taped the Pamper mold in place. I had guessed the general hoof size pretty accurately. The duct tape was perfect for molding and securing the Pampers in place.

"We won't force him up," Burton said. "When he's ready, he'll stand."

He stood watching Sheridan for a moment. I sat near his head, scratching him behind his ears. He lifted his head, tucking his front legs beneath him, and nosing at my pocket where he knew my carrots resided.

I gave him a handful.

"He sure is a good-natured fellow," Burton said. "You would never think a horse that had suffered so much at the hands of humans would trust them again."

Sheridan must have decided he wanted to give his new hoof covers a try, because he gathered his legs and heaved himself up. I scrambled out of the way. When he stood, he shook his mane, and sighed deeply.

Burton chuckled. "That almost sounded like a sigh of relief. I think your contraption might help."

"I'll ice his hooves now," I said.

"I don't imagine you'll have to do that much longer," Burton said. "Dr. Creola said the swelling is going down, and the abscess is almost totally drained. Maybe only another week of those nasty maggots."

That would be a delight! I didn't mind all the work icing Sheridan, or keeping his stall spotless, or replacing his thick bedding. But it did take time away from Gidget, and I missed her.

She always waited patiently, and didn't seem perturbed that our time together was in brief snatches between the icing periods with Sheridan. It was almost as though she understood, and even approved.

The only riding I did was in the pasture. After my quick training sessions with Trinity, I often hopped on Gidget's back, using her mane to tug and guide her. It wasn't as exciting as going out on the trail, but it was magical in its own way.

I think those brief sessions riding tack-free across the pasture were building her trust. Those times were usually uneventful, and oftentimes I lay across her back and let her go wherever she wanted to while I sang to her.

Putting the brakes on my day-dreaming, I returned to my horsey sick-bay duties. I dumped ice from a small freezer in the tack room into my home-made ice wrap. While Sheridan munched his morning hay, I tied the ice bags around his hooves.

At this moment, Mick peeked over the stall door.

"Dad said you found an ingenious use for diapers. I'd always assumed you'd have mastered potty training by now."

I ignored him, and continued setting the icebags in place.

"Clever!" he said, looking down at Sheridan's feet. "Now when all those maggots poop, they don't need to be ashamed."

I stood up.

"Do you ever get tired of making fun of me?" I asked.

Mick thought for a moment. "Nope."

I petted Sheridan's nose and started to slip out of the stall.

"He's feeling better," Mick said. "He's probably starting to get bored standing or lying in his stall all day. You need to spice up his life."

"How?" I asked, "He can't exercise yet."

"You could put his hay in a hay bag so he has to work to get it out. Gives him something to do."

I had never heard of a hay bag. Mick explained it was just a mesh bag that you tied to the stall after filling it with hay.

"It's not as challenging as, say, taking a class in calculus but for a horse, it keeps their mind busy trying to pick the hay out of the bag."

"Where do I get one?" I asked.

"If you are clever enough to make booties out of Pampers, I imagine you can devise how to make a hay bag. Use the bale twine. We have plenty."

Sheridan popped his nose over the door. To my disbelief, Mick stroked it.

"I have an idea," he said. "I thought of a way to nail that trainer at Heritage. It is actually Fiora's idea."

Fiora! Any idea from Fiora probably involved things that would make me blush (not that that was difficult).

"He's working with another Tennessee Walker. This one is at a farm over in Lombard. Fiora knows when the next big show is because her dad enters horses in all of them. We just need to get an inspector to that show."

"She should be sending the inspector to catch her dad," I said.

"She is. That's part of her plan."

I leaned back against the stall door. Much as I hated Fiora, I couldn't imagine how hard it must be to turn your own dad over to authorities that could ruin his career. If he couldn't work, how could he buy her those threads she called clothes?

"Isn't she worried he'll lose his job if he's fined?"

"She doesn't care. She doesn't live there anymore anyway."

"Where does she live? With her mom?"

"Nope. Her mom's dead."

"Oh." Bella had been right! "Well who takes care of her?"

"No one. She lives in the forest by the trail."

I stared at him. Was he kidding? She did always seem to pop out of the same spot in the forest. It never occurred to me she might be homeless.

"What does she do in the winter?" I asked.

"She only left when she turned 16," he said, "This summer. She hasn't figured out a cold weather plan yet."

"Didn't her dad try to find her?" This was so far outside my experience, that I couldn't begin to wrap my head around it. Mick had told me many times my lack of comprehension was understandable because *no way* could such a small skull wrap itself around anything.

"He kicked her out."

I blinked, astonished.

"Why?"

"She threatened to expose the soring. He told her he'd kill her if she did that."

"Well if he's caught, he'll know she did it."

"That's why she wants you to call the inspectors."

"What about you? Why should *I* get killed?"

"If I call, and he finds out, Dad will be black-listed as a farrier. He needs the work. You heard Mr. Banks. He already threatened Dad if he squealed about Sheridan."

"Someone has to stop them," I said.

Mick nodded, looking at me. "Someone with the least reason to live."

I squeezed past him, heading to the tack room. "I'll think about it. Get me the information. I'm gonna go work with Gidget."

"Well while you are frying your brain trying to turn it on, here is another problem. Fiora said that the reason the trainers are so hard to catch is they know when they government inspectors are there. They just don't unload their horses, when they see the inspectors. They turn around and go home, and wait for the second day of the show. They say the inspectors never show up two days in a row."

I turned to look at him. "How could anyone be so evil?"

Mick met my gaze and surprised me. "I don't know. Sheridan didn't deserve it. He's such a nice horse." He was still stroking Sheridan's nose as I gathered my tack and headed off to the pasture.

Chapter Nine

As I lunged Trinity, I thought about what Mick had said. Surely, I would be in no danger contacting an inspector. How would it ever be traced back to me? Of course, how could I prove anything against the trainer without mentioning Sheridan? I hadn't seen any of the other horses he worked with. But if the abusive trainers just turned around and refused to unload the show horses when the inspectors were there, how would they ever be caught?

Besides, the only one that was in a position to report the abuse with any kind of evidence was Fiora. The wood nymph.

I needed to talk with Bella about Fiora. How was she surviving? What was she eating? Was she really living all alone in the forest? Why had Mick kept that a secret? It was possible he was making the whole thing up. He loved seeing how gullible I could be, which was, in a word, *very*.

If it was as simple as reporting a suspected soring trainer, then wouldn't they be caught all the time? No. Mick told me that if

I just reported it to the show officials, they would likely provide a veterinarian from the industry rather than a government inspector. "According to Fiora, those vets are paid or coerced to overlook violations. As Tennessee Walking Horse vets, they benefit from the popularity of the *big lick* horses. It's like the fox guarding the hen-house, though in your case," Mick said, "It is like the brain guarding the idea. If you had any…"

"I *do* have an idea!" I snapped at him. He had wandered onto the field where I was working with Trinity.

"Stop the presses!"

"Why don't the inspectors come at the *end* of the show? After the horse wins? I mean, the most likely horse to win would be a sored horse, right?"

Mick considered this. "I almost think you may have stumbled on a decent thought. There isn't much money for the government inspectors. Fiora told me they don't have nearly enough funds to show up at every show. They only come to very few. We'd have to find a way to lure them to the show Fiora knows they're competing in."

"Then tell Fiora we need evidence. I am willing to call the inspectors but I need evidence. We can give her Bella's camera."

"I already took pictures. Any of those pictures could be described as something else. None prove the horses were sored."

"Half the pictures were of the Banks' daughter," I pointed out. After Bella had taken the film to be developed, two things were clear. First, we both agreed the Banks' girl was quite pretty. Secondly, the other pictures were not incriminating enough to nail Banks' sorry hide.

"Was Bella jealous when she saw them?" he asked hopefully.

I rolled my eyes. "Glad you're so invested in helping the horses." Milly called to Mick, needing help with the trail horses. He dashed away.

I knew *I* would not have the courage to call the inspectors, even if I could figure out who to call. But Miss Scruggs would have the courage! I was almost certain she would help me. Maybe it was a lousy idea, but it was the only one I had.

When I finished working with Trinity, Dr. Creola was standing in the aisle looking in on Sheridan. Sheridan was still upright!

"Those Pamper boots look mighty comfy," Dr. Creola said. "That was a good idea."

His praise melted over me, oozing balm over the fissures that shy, frizzy-haired girls accumulate in their psyches. At least, this one did.

"I think we can start very limited walking with him. Maybe while wearing those clever booties you made for him. The blood circulation would be good for the laminae. We need to be careful not to overdo it."

"OK," I said, "How far should I go?"

"Just take him to the water trough in the yard for now. We'll see how he handles that short walk. I think with how far the swelling is reduced, you can decrease icing. Maybe just when you feed him now."

I snapped a lead rope to his halter, and gently tugged to urge him out of the stall. He paused briefly, looking at me as though to assess what would happen if he didn't move. I knew the trainer had beat him when he balked because of the pain in his legs. I reached into my pocket, to gather carrots, and he flinched.

Poor baby. He was expecting *even me* to beat him. "It's ok," I cooed in a quiet voice, stroking his nose, and opening a fistful of carrots to him. He gobbled them up, and when I moved forward again, he followed me.

He walked slowly, and a little gingerly, but he wasn't grunting in pain like when we had first walked him into his stall. At the water trough, he took a long, deep drink, and then lifted his beautiful head and looked all around. It was the first time he'd been outdoors in two weeks.

"Can we put him in the round pen do you think?" I asked Dr.Creola. "It looks like he is enjoying the sun."

Dr. Creola agreed that would be all right. He didn't think Sheridan was inclined to move more than he had to, and he did seem happy in the fresh, warm summer air.

Sheridan followed me slowly, looking around with interest. When we reached the pen, I unsnapped the lead and closed the gate behind him. He stretched his neck across the gate, gazing at the herd in the pasture. Gidget had seen me, and was trotting to the fence closest to the pen. She raised her head high, silvery mane and tail streaming behind her. Sheridan whinnied, and she nickered in response.

"Oh-oh. They're in love." I swung around at the unexpected voice. It was Fiora. "If you all plan on keeping him, don't forget he's a stallion. Has anyone considered that?"

I hadn't. But she raised an interesting point. He was a beautiful Tennessee Walking Horse. People paid to have offspring from champions, and he had been a promising show horse.

I still didn't speak. I had no idea of what to say to her. All I could think of was that she had no mother, and probably no breakfast. What had she been eating in the woods? Acorns? But I didn't dare ask her.

"You're Miss Motor-Mouth, aren't you?" she asked.

Gidget had reached the fence now, tossing her head. She looked like she was showing off for Sheridan. I didn't blame her. He was such a stunner. He forgot the pain in his legs, and paced back and forth along the fence.

"Is he wearing diapers on his hooves?" she asked.

I laughed. "Yeah...it seems to make him feel better."

She shook her head, chuckling. "Now that's a first."

We watched him stride along the fence, shaking his head as though mimicking Gidget.

"They make a cute couple," she said.

I could stand the suspense no longer. "Fiora, what are you doing here?"

She shrugged. "I thought I'd come help out."

Despite her scanty clothes, and lewd hip motion, she looked vulnerable for a moment. I may have imagined it, now knowing about her mother and background with her dad. Something compelled me to be kind to her, which was not at all my first impulse with her.

"Have you had lunch? My mom packed double and I am just going to throw it out otherwise."

She gazed at me. "Mick told you, didn't he?"

"Yes."

"I don't need your pity."

"I'm not offering pity. Just a bologna and peanut butter sandwich."

Her eyebrows raised and she burst into laughter. "That's my favorite! I didn't know anyone else made that!"

"I get made fun of for it a lot," I admitted.

"Well, yeah. I'll take it if you are really just going to throw it out."

"Wait here, and I'll get it out of the tack room fridge. Watch Sheridan. I don't think he should move around much more. This is his first time out of the stall."

I was glad Mick was nowhere in sight. My guess is he was on a trail ride. The usual mob of horses along the fence was gone. They must have departed while I was working with Trinity.

I handed Fiora my lunch bag. I didn't need lunch that one day. Maybe it would help equalize the size of my thighs with my head.

"I have an idea about how to nail that trainer at Heritage," I said.

"I thought you would come up with something. His name is Bob Mortis, by the way."

"I don't know if it will work. I know the trainers won't show when government inspectors are there before the show. If you can tell me the class and show that Sheridan's trainer will be in, I was hoping to get an inspector to show up after the class."

"Good luck. There isn't much money for the inspection program. They show up at very few shows. And believe me, every *big lick* horse has been sored. The inspectors know they will find violations at every show."

"What if I had proof?"

"Dream on. This has been going on for decades. *Big lick* horses are big money. So far, nothing has put a dent in the soring, even though some people have spoken out. My dad threatened to kill me if I talked about what he did. Touching, isn't it, a father's love? I don't know what kind of proof you think you can get."

"Mick got some pictures."

"Pictures won't be enough. Someone would have to be willing to talk. Someone involved with him. Someone who knows what he's doing."

I sighed, the feeble wisp of hope I'd had dissipated. Fiora finished the sandwich and then reached in the lunch bag. A Little Debbie! I didn't know Mom had packed that rare treat.

I tried not to drool as Fiora crinkled open the tasty morsel.

"You sure you don't want this?" she asked.

"I'm sure," I lied. It was gone in three bites.

"Do you have something warm to wear at night?" I asked. Nights were cool, even in the summer.

She licked the last bit off chocolate off her lips, and wiped her mouth with the back of a less than completely clean hand. "I'm fine. I've got friends."

"Maybe your father misses you…" I said.

"Yeah, like he misses a kick in the $$#$%^^&**." She swore with vehemence, but her eyes were sad. I couldn't imagine being on my own with no one to care for or love me.

"I gotta go," she said. "I'll think about your idea of proof. The show is at the Dupage County Fairgrounds, August 23rd. It's the last show near here before the big Celebration national show in Shelbyville, Tennessee. You can't imagine all the horror that must have gone down for those horses to get that far."

"Will your dad be at the Dupage show?"

"Yes. All the TWH from this area will be there. It is the last qualifier for the national show."

"Then the inspectors would be there, wouldn't they?"

"Maybe. No one is keen on ruining the historic Shelbyville Celebration. They can't celebrate without the big name horses."

"Is *every* big name horse sored? Aren't some of them just naturally high steppers like that?"

Fiora tossed her flaming red hair out her eyes, and glared at me with disdain. "Sure. Just like Sheridan."

She looked disgusted, as she tossed my empty lunch bag at my feet. Swirling around, she jogged back towards the trail and the forest. The shadows from the overhanging leafy trees swallowed her whole.

Chapter Ten

When I told Bella all I had learned, her eyes watered. "That poor girl. I knew something was up with her parents."

It's true. She *had* known somehow about the dead mother.

"We have to help her." Bella squared her shoulders, and stood tall, defiant.

I scowled at my friend. "How can we help her? And besides, my hands are full trying to help Sheridan, and to figure out how to catch Bob Mortis."

"We can't just ignore it now that we know Fiora has no home... and no mother."

I sighed. It was no use fighting Bella. If she was determined to do good, she would not rest till it was accomplished. Besides, the no-mother bit really tugged on her own wounded heart strings. It would take less effort just to deal with the Fiora distraction now and get it over with.

"Maybe her father isn't so terrible. Maybe she ran away so she could run around half naked and meet boys in the forest."

"Maybe. We need to find out," Bella said.

This was getting more ridiculous by the second. We were two fourteen-year-old girls. Not only was Bella certain I could bring down an entire horse industry's abusive practice, but that I could repair the relationship of a troubled runaway and her criminal father.

"I think you are confusing me with someone else you know...like *God*," I said.

She smiled at me. "Well, we *are* to be the hands and feet of Jesus. But actually, I was thinking this is something my dad could help with. Our church works with lots of agencies that help abused kids and at-risk families."

Well that was a relief.

She brought me to Mr. Temple, and I told him everything I knew about Fiora. I tried to keep the account strictly factual and left out subjective observations like *street-walking tart*.

He said he would take over from here. I felt a little bad, since I knew Social Services would not let a 16-year-old girl live on her own in the forest. I suspected Fiora would be hopping mad if she figured out I had anything to do with whatever Mr. Temple devised to help her.

Fortunately, Bella didn't mention any of our plans regarding the soring trainers. I knew I wasn't doing anything dangerous (yet) but I didn't think Mr. Temple needed to worry about us any more than necessary.

The next morning, I stopped off at the Community Library before heading to Burton's Farm. Bella promised me that she would go and ice Sheridan's hooves for me during the morning feeding. She said if she had any trouble, Mick would probably agree to help her. Since I knew Mick would try to lasso Jupiter if Bella requested it, I was confident Sheridan would be in good hands.

Miss Scruggs was surprised to see me, since I almost never went to the library during summer days except Sundays. I spent every other waking moment at the farm.

"What brings you out here?" she asked.

"Remember that terrible training used with Tennessee Walking Horses that we read about?"

"Yes. It was very sad."

"I think I know a way to help. But I don't think anyone will listen to me since I am just a kid."

"How can I help?" she asked instantly. See? That's why I loved Miss Scruggs so much. Maybe not all librarians are cream of the crop human beings like Miss Scruggs, though I bet most are.

"I want to report a trainer to the inspectors. I know he will be bringing sore horses to the Dupage County show."

"How do you know that?"

"I don't think I can tell you. Someone told me, but I can't give her name or she will get in a lot of trouble."

"Hmmm. Do you have any proof?"

"I have some photographs, but I don't know if they will be enough."

"May I see them?"

I pulled the prints out of my pocket. They were not the greatest pictures. Mick had taken far more care with the photos of the Banks' daughter. To be fair, he had to photograph Sheridan under cover.

Miss Scruggs spread the pictures out. There was one of Sheridan's pasterns wrapped with the tape, the heavy chains, and the heavy shoes.

"These are illegal?" she asked.

"No."

She startled, covering her mouth with her hand. "It is *legal* for the horses to wear shoes like this? They look tortuous."

"That's how I feel," I said.

The next picture was of him lying down. The third was of him being pulled up by the trainer, whip in hand. I wondered how Mick had gotten that one.

"None of these show him in the act of being abused," I said sadly.

"This is the horse you are helping?"

I nodded.

"Do you have pictures of damage to his feet?"

Stupido! I didn't. We should have been taking pictures of Dr. Creola's treatment all along. A picture of a maggot filled abscess was worth a thousand words. Why had that not occurred to me?

Miss Scruggs knew the answer from the expression on my face, and hugged me. "Oh sweetie. Don't worry. He's not recovered yet, is he? Get the pictures now. And have you asked the vet to describe what he has seen?"

No. Again, I smacked my head. Burton had been threatened not to breathe a word about Sheridan's abuse, but no one had told Dr. Creola not to. I hadn't thought to ask Dr. Creola to help us. I couldn't believe that obvious oversight.

"If your vet will provide a written statement with these pictures, and pictures of the injury…I think we have good evidence to bring to the inspectors."

I felt like an ignoramus for not thinking of such an obvious solution myself, but the first bit of hope pirouetted over the whole soring debacle. At least if I was an idiot, I was smart enough to have a friend like Miss Scruggs.

"There is one Gordian Knot."

I loved that Miss Scruggs used fantastic words like Gordian Knot with me. She was a walking vocabulary lesson. I waited to hear what the Gordian Knot was.

"This only proves the trainer abused *Sheridan*. It doesn't prove he abused the horse he is bringing to the show."

And that was a huge problem since according to the law, soring itself wasn't illegal. Only showing or transporting a sored horse was against the law.

"After we report him, we may want to write our congressman," she added. "Like why would a shoe like this be allowed in the first place? Or chains? And why isn't the whole practice of soring outlawed?"

I hugged Miss Scruggs, even though I am not normally a hugging type of person. I left the pictures for her to make copies, and she promised to find a name and number to call to report the soring, and would ask for the inspector to visit the show. Meanwhile I was in charge of new pictures of Sheridan's wounded sole, and the testimony from Dr. Creola.

I was lucky that Dr. Creola was there when I arrived. He brought Tara so that she could work with me and Trinity. I planned to let her hold the lunge line for the first time. She was bouncing up and down with excitement, but I told her to go feed the chickens while I talked with her dad.

First, I told Dr. Creola what Miss Scruggs and I discussed. He put his hand on my shoulder and told me, "You are doing a good thing. I would be honored to help."

We unwrapped Sheridan's Pamper/towel bootie. Dr. Creola held his hoof still while I was the lucky one to snap some photos of the squirming, disgusting maggots in the abscessed sole. I had purposely avoided looking at that portion of his treatment, and came pretty close to losing my lunch (which would have been a tragedy since Mom had packed Little Debbies again)!

Dr. Creola told me that while I was working with Trinity, he would write a statement for Miss Scruggs and include his contact information.

"You tell her that if they want me to testify against this man, I am willing to do so."

Tara and I gathered our tack for lunging Trinity. The day had already been eventful. I didn't need the sight that greeted me next. Gidget was in her usual corner, but lying down. I was not alarmed until she rolled as though to stand, then flopped over again.

I dropped the tack and sprinted towards her, shouting to Tara to get her father. When I drew near, I knew right away what was happening. I'd seen it before. Gidget was miscarrying. This time, instead of one foal, it was clear that twin foals were lying dead in the bloody sac near her tail.

Later, Dr. Creola told me that some horses, like some people, are prone to carrying twins. It was not at all uncommon for horses to miscarry foals, especially twins. He examined Gidget afterwards, and told me she would be fine. He patted my back and told me she was a healthy young horse, and this didn't mean she could not have other foals one day.

Mick was not yet back from leading a trail. I dreaded telling him. He had been so excited about finally owning and training his own horse. It had been crucial in healing the guilt and sadness he felt over his deceased brother, and the colt he'd loved during that hard time in his life. Sadly, now there was no foal.

Poor Gidget seemed sad too. She leaned her head against me afterwards, and didn't move. She just stood there while I hugged her and told her how sorry I was. Dr. Creola led Tara away and left us alone. I sang one of our favorite songs to Gidget which was appropriate to the moment, *You'll Never Walk Alone.* Her tail swished in time to my words of comfort, but otherwise, she was motionless.

That's how Mick found us. His face looked as stricken as Gidget's. Probably mine too, but I couldn't see my own face.

I looked up when I heard his footsteps.

"I'm sorry, Mick."

He squeezed his lips in a tight, straight line. He stopped at Gidget's neck and patted her. Then he leaned his forehead against her and shut his eyes.

"I really wanted this foal," he said finally.

Mick never stopped joking and taunting. I waited to see if he would follow with some spiteful comment, some sarcastic way of blaming me for this. I wouldn't have minded. I was on to him, now, and understood where his venom came from. I didn't really mind any more since I knew the source of his nastiness had nothing to do with me.

However, that was all he said. He stood there with his head against her neck, arms straight at his side. I remained silent. I certainly wasn't going to sing to him, though he looked like he could use an inspiring message.

"Sometimes, life sucks." With this pronouncement, he patted Gidget again, and walked away, back towards the barn.

Chapter Eleven

With icing duties reduced to just twice a day, and Sheridan slowly improving, I was able to resume trail leading with Gidget. There was a month of summer left and then its end would coincide roughly with the Dupage County show.

Miss Scruggs told me she had called the federal inspection hotline, and read Dr. Creola's statement over the phone. She described the photos and shared our idea of them coming after Bob Mortis' class to inspect his horse. She told me they thanked her for the information, and assured her they would do their best. With the important national show at Shelbyville coming up, they could not promise they could be at the Dupage show. Limited funds forced them to pick and choose which shows they could monitor.

Miss Scruggs told me she had done her best and now the rest was up to God. Bella said, "Amen" when I relayed the conversation to her.

"If I were God, I would long ago have sent a lightning bolt through every soring trainer's heart," I said. I probably shouldn't have said that, but I couldn't help it.

"I don't blame you," Bella said, "That's how I feel too. Maybe that's why we're not God. The Bible says *vengeance is the Lord's and he will repay.*"

"When?"

"He doesn't tell us that."

"I hope it is on August 23rd."

Dr. Creola's bill would wipe out all my savings, but I knew that he had given us a cut rate. He was there nearly every day the first month of Sheridan's recovery. Burton told me we had dodged a bullet that the laminitis had not become founder.

By the way, maybe some of you are as clueless as I was about those conditions. Laminitis is when the soft tissue (the laminae) that attaches the hoof wall to the horses "coffin" bone in the foot becomes inflamed. The coffin bone is the main weight bearing bone in the horse foot. I wondered why it was called the coffin bone, but even Miss Scruggs couldn't tell me.

I assume it is because if a horse injures the coffin bone, he may need a coffin. It is a *seriously* important bone to preserve. Laminitis is very painful and it can affect the structural integrity of the coffin bone. The reason Bob Mortis was so eager to get rid of Sheridan once he heard the word laminitis is that laminitis can be managed if caught early enough, but not cured...and the horse will always be susceptible to future bouts. If the laminae continue to degrade, then it leads to the more serious condition of founder. Most horses that develop founder need to be euthanized. Dr. Creola told me we had caught Sheridan just in time.

Laminitis takes several months to heal well enough for most horses to be allowed to exercise at anything approaching a normal level. Some horses would never reach any level of soundness. Some would have to be euthanized even after all the work to restore their hooves. That was a depressing bit of news, and Miss Scruggs was nearby when I read that in the reference book at the library. She came rushing over because I started hyperventilating in an attempt to keep from screaming unspeakable things out loud about Bob Mortis.

In the first month of laminitis recovery, the only exercise should be self-induced by the horse, and he should be restricted in any exercise during acute pain. This is of course the opposite of what the sorers do to the poor horse! Bob Mortis knew that to get the *big lick* step, he had to continue with the obscene heavy "pressure shoes," and they would only make the laminitis worse.

He didn't give us Sheridan out of any humane impulse. He had a problem and saw us as a cheap way to eliminate it. I didn't share with Bella what I would have done to Bob Mortis if I were a superhero like Batman. I *did* tell Miss Scruggs as she was calming me down, and she said she would have helped me.

As the horse recovered, balanced trimming and shoeing was important. Dr. Creola and Burton spent a lot of time going over what was necessary for Sheridan. Burton never charged me for his farrier work. That was a bonus. I could never have afforded it. He was trimming Sheridan's hooves and shaping them once every three weeks! I really had no idea exactly what he did that was helping Sheridan's normal hoof growth, but he smiled more and more as the weeks progressed when he checked Sheridan's hooves.

The frequent sessions of trimming during the first few weeks of the acute painful phase would be reduced as Sheridan healed, Burton told me. I didn't understand most of what he was doing, but it had something to do with adjusting how the weight was distributed so that the coffin bone didn't distort or shift position and the stress was taken off the laminae. I had no idea Burton knew anything about any of this. I suspect he was learning as he was going along, but Dr. Creola told me that without Burton, Sheridan would not have pulled through.

"Dad's still a ###@$%^&**," Mick told me, though he admitted he was "less so." While Mick's usual antagonism was no surprise, his constant presence and help while Burton worked on Sheridan *was*. I even caught him reading a manual on hoof anatomy that Burton kept near to guide him in his work on Sheridan. When Mick was helping one day, I saw Burton smiling at him in a way I'd never seen…as though with a mix of pride and even *love*.

Fortunately, Dr. Creola's $10 a week payment to me for working with Tara and Trinity covered the cost of hay for Sheridan with some left over. The problem would be in the winter. I couldn't imagine poor Sheridan would be ready to brave the Illinois winter without a stall. How could I cover the cost of a stall?

Bella told me, "Today has enough problems of its own. Don't borrow tomorrow's trouble."

"God again?" I asked.

"God again."

"Is there any situation he doesn't cover?"

"Not that I have found."

I asked Dr. Creola when or even *if* Sheridan could ever be ridden again. He said he felt very confident that Sheridan would be able to return to normal riding activities by the end of the year. "He will always have to be monitored for laminitis, but he is over the worst of it already."

Thus, with Sheridan able to be left alone for longer periods, I was ready and eager to resume my trail duties. Bella had ridden Skippy at the end of Mick's trail rides a few times by now, and was becoming a competent trail follower. I was so excited that my best friend would now be my assistant when I led the trails. Our first time out together on a trail, me at the head, she at the tail, was one of the happiest days of my life. If you, like most normal people have had a lifetime of friends, you wouldn't understand.

I put the hackamore on Gidget, and heaved myself onto her back. Mick was grumpy as he helped the trail riders onto their mounts. He shot a quick look at my graceless mounting technique, and asked if I planned to go out for the USA gymnastics team with my "abundance of acrobatic skill."

Bella could get on Skippy all by herself now, which wasn't super hard since Skippy was a small pony. Mick smiled at her and told her she was "truly a gift to the equine community." Bella flicked her eyes at me, and I could tell she was suppressing giggles.

I reined Gidget towards the trail head. She darted a look at the round pen, where Sheridan was getting his daily dose of sun and limited exercise. He called out to her, with a trumpeting whinny, and she whinnied in return. I was glad my two favorite horses liked each other.

The trail horses all clip-clopped in my wake as we started along the edge of the Narroway Highway. This was the worst part of the whole trail ride, but was fortunately not a very long segment. The traffic noise was not pleasant, and there was always the chance of some idiot blowing his car horn while passing us, and spooking the horses.

Since I knew this was a possibility, I always had my reins gathered and was alert to Gidget's body language. This particular day, she was relaxed. She was doubly as spry as any of the other horses at Burton's Farm, but I was by now an experienced rider, and almost never lost control of her.

I turned to check the line of riders.

"Everyone okay back there?" I called.

"All is well!" Bella replied.

We passed the spot where Fiora had popped out of the forest in the past. No Fiora this time. Mr. Temple had contacted Social Services with the information I had given him. They had canvassed the whole area and no one could find her. They phoned Mr. Heller, her father, who said he hadn't seen her since she left to move in with her grandmother. That was the first I had heard of the grandmother!

The grandmother knew nothing about Fiora's intentions to move in with her, and in fact called her a little "no good whore," which I thought was harsh of Grammy. As I passed the spot in the forest, I felt guilty. Where *was* Fiora, then? Had I unwittingly made her plight worse?

Our little line of trail riders plodded along as the sun brandished its golden paintbrush. *If I could be on a horse's back every moment, would I have a sunnier personality?* I tended to be melancholy, and obsessed at times over the sadness of the world. At least of *my* world. I cried when I saw dead squirrels in the road or even dead beetles on the sidewalk. Trust me, that type of hyper-sensitivity to suffering was not an easy characteristic to bear day in and day out.

Gidget's head dipped and rose with each clomp of her hoof on the sun-hardened trail. Silence reigned, except for the steady beats of the horses' hooves behind us. The soothing cadence lulled me into dreamy musings.

Dr. Creola was so pleased with Sheridan's progress that he felt we could start some longer sessions walking. He didn't want Sheridan to be ridden yet, but felt by the end of the summer, even that was a possibility on a very limited basis. He said the recovery was near-miraculous. Unlike Bella, who attributed it to God, Dr.Creola said that certainly may have played a part, but the disgusting maggots deserved some credit.

"Well," Bella said, when I told her what Dr. Creola felt was the source of Sheridan's astounding progress, "*God* created the maggots."

"I never thought I would thank Him for maggots," I agreed. "Who would have thought a creature of so much torment, like the fly, could be the source of healing?"

Bella *naturally* pounced right on that. "There's a verse in the Bible…"

Of course there was….

"What you meant for harm, God meant it for good."

I considered that verse now, as the gentle rocking of Gidget's gait filled me with peace. All the terrible things that had happened to Sheridan were definitely evil. He had suffered greatly, and Bob Mortis should pay for that. However, now Sheridan was leading a cushy, happy life and I finally had a horse of my own.

Gidget- the Horse That Waited For Me

Now it is true he was a great horse, but he *wasn't* the horse I *really* wanted. Gidget had noodled her way deep into my heart, and I still saw no way that I could ever own her. And now that she was no longer pregnant, I knew her days with Burton's Farm were numbered. She was a wonderful horse, but she was not a trail horse. Too flighty and unpredictable for novice riders, although not with me. With her beauty and youth, and half-Arabian bloodlines, someone who was a great equestrian would buy her and pay decent money too. My beloved Gidget's days at Burton's Farm were coming to an end, and I had no idea how to prevent that.

The trail horses slogged on, uneventfully. We came to the trotting section of the trail. On occasion, one of the novice trail riders tumbled off their mount during this segment. It was almost hoped-for, since it livened up the day. It was boring when nothing out of the ordinary happened on the back to back trail rides I led. I was slated to lead three in a row that afternoon!

"Get ready to trot!" I called back to the riders. A few of them clutched their horses' manes, and clenched their teeth.

"Nothing to worry about!" Bella said with her usual bonhomie and chirpy optimism, "Trotting is fun!"

I squeezed my heels into Gidget's sides, and she instantly sprang forward. I loved her spirit and energy. The horses behind me were less immediately compliant, and I heard Bella urging the riders to kick their horses' sides.

I remembered how hesitant I had been to kick my mount when I was first learning to ride. It seemed cruel. Since then, I'd learned that the Burton Farm nags would not give trotting a moment's thought unless strongly induced to do so. Nothing but kicking them woke them from their trail ride nap.

Eventually, the line-up of seven horses were all in bouncy motion, and every rider was clinging to the saddle horn, while heads snapped about on their necks like bobble-head dolls. We reached the top of the hill, and I slowed Gidget to a walk.

"Everyone still on board?" I asked, turning to glance at my group.

They all nodded and some gave me a thumb's up. Bella waved at me, beaming with happiness. Her feet were just inches from the ground. I thought it might be time to suggest she move to a bigger mount.

What sounded like a loud mosquito buzzed in the distance, and a puff of dirt spiraled in the air just past the tree line. The buzz grew louder and a dirt bike materialized, heading towards us. I knew dirt bikes sometimes roared along our trails, but they were not supposed to. Signs posted all along the state property warned that motorized vehicles were not permitted. Several farms backed up to the forest, and trail horses often used the paths.

I flapped my arms at the dirt biker, and signaled for him to move away. He didn't see me, or ignored me. I can't imagine he didn't see the long line of horses. It's not like they are small mammals.

When he did decide to veer away, the damage was done. Gidget had never seen a dirt bike, and while I had already gathered the reins and tried to quiet her nervous prancing, her old spookishness returned with a vengeance.

She shot forward, neck high, fighting the reins. The dirt biker seemed to find the runaway horse hilarious, and revved his engine. That was all the other horses needed to deduce that the sky was falling, and they all stampeded after me.

I see-sawed at the reins, calling, "Hooooo Gidget, hooooo!"

At a sharp curve in the trail, she swerved. Since she was momentarily caught off balance, I managed to turn her head sharply. I crashed against her neck, but stayed on, and she came to a skidding stop, still snorting and tossing her head against the reins. She spun like a top in a tight circle. Until either dizzy or tired, she sputtered to a wheezing halt.

This was one of the rare times when a runaway group managed to all stop without a single rider crashing to the ground. Even Bella, riding her first canter bareback, remained successfully perched atop Skippy.

The group huffed and puffed, and gathered behind me. They milled about with varying degrees of horror on their faces.

"Everyone did great!" Bella said.

I nodded, still breathless. I was sorry Gidget had shied, but this was the first time I had been able to bring her back under control. It could have been a disaster if she had continued running. There would have been casualties for sure, and she would have sealed Burton's decision to sell her.

"Was that a gallop?" one of the riders asked.

"It was faster than a gallop," one of the kids said. "I want to do that again."

"Once is enough excitement for me," his mother countered.

Me too. I waited till everyone had calmed down, and the horses' snorting and heavy spurts of air from flared nostrils had moderated. Bella, with her usual perfect timing, told the group the story of her first time when a group had stampeded like that and how nearly everyone fell off.

By the time she was finished, every rider felt like they were the most talented new trail riders on the planet since not a single person had fallen off their horse. Bella always had that effect on people.

When we returned to the farm, Milly helped the riders dismount. "How was your ride?" she asked.

The woman who had not wanted a repeat gallop took a breath to answer. I winced.

"Your leader is a wonderful trail guide," she said. "Some crazy kid on a motorbike spooked the horses, and she was able to stop her horse, who twirled around in just the perfect place to bring all the other horses under control. We will come again, and we want her for our guide."

I almost fell off of Gidget. No one had ever, *not ever*, praised my horse skills or my horse. It had really been an accident that I had managed to control Gidget or that she had spun around in a way that made the other horses unable to pass her.

"That was no accident," Bella told me as we walked home together.

"God again?" I asked.

"God again."

I nodded thoughtfully. "Your God sure gets around.

Chapter Twelve

My birthday arrived, and I turned fifteen-years-old. My parents wrote me a gift check that would cover the rest of the year's hay for Sheridan. I hadn't confided in them about the problem of paying for a stall. I was taking Bella's advice, and leaving tomorrow's problem for tomorrow. I was afraid if they started adding up all the costs, my brief foray into owning a horse would be over.

Trinity was now a year old. I had at least another year with her, so I could count on $40 a month from Dr. Creola. That was enough for a stall, especially with the cost of the hay now covered. As long as Sheridan stayed sound, and there were no vet bills, I could maybe swing it. He had warned me they would need one more x-ray to be sure Sheridan's bones had not drifted about during his treatment. I didn't dare ask if that would put me over my $300 budget, but he assured me my money would cover everything.

Milly had not talked with me at all about boarding costs for Sheridan's stall. Right now, she didn't even have a stall open.

Sheridan was using Trinity's stall while the weather was so perfect. Kind as Dr. Creola was, I doubted he would give me Trinity's stall during the harsh winter months.

But I dashed those woebegone thoughts aside and held my breath as Dr. Creola watched Burton remove the padding around Sheridan's left hoof. Mick was assisting Burton, handing tools as needed. He was watching with interest. I could not watch, though I *was* interested. And to be clear, I was not holding my breath merely from anticipation. I also knew that when the padding came off, sometimes the stink from the abscessed sole was *not* like honeysuckles and ivory soap.

The changing of the maggots was always a time of high drama. It had been nearly two months now, and the maggots had gotten skinnier and skinnier with each change. This time, as Dr. Creola helped Burton clean out the much smaller hole in the sole, all that fell out were emaciated, dead maggots.

"Poor things," Mick said with a smirk, "Nothing left for them to eat."

"We can officially call the maggot therapy at an end." Dr.Creola held one of the deceased maggots in his finger tips for all to see. I swallowed bile rising in my gut.

To reduce the trauma to Sheridan's healing hooves, Burton would use some special glue to secure his new shoes in place. First, Dr. Creola cleaned the whole area, and examined the laminae. He pronounced them "remarkably normal."

Sheridan was off all pain-killers now, and Dr. Creola felt the antibiotics could be stopped as well. Burton would continue with careful, regular hoof shaping and shoeing, but the medical phase of Sheridan's recovery was coming to an end.

I breathed a sigh of relief, since I was the one funding the medical bill. Mick glanced at me, and grinned.

"You should come see this, since it's your horse," he said, "It's good to know what a healthy hoof looks like."

"Not till you sweep up the maggots," I said. I had faithfully gathered the maggots for two months. I never wanted to see another maggot in my lifetime, grateful as I was to them for their service.

"They deserve a burial with full honors," Dr. Creola said. "I am convinced they are the reason Sheridan has done so well."

I tip-toed over to Sheridan's side. Burton kneeled with the hoof turned up between his legs.

"Show her the parts, Mick," he said. I thought for a moment Mick was going to say something nasty, but then he looked at his father. Burton was smiling at him, and nodded.

"Ok. This here is called the frog." Mick pointed to the middle section that was triangular, tip pointing to the front of the hoof.

"Why?" I asked.

"Why what?"

"Why is it called a frog?"

Mick *hated* my interest in etymology. Miss Scruggs would have patted my head and answered with enthusiasm.

"Probably because we all will *croak* trying to tell you about all the horse parts if you have to know why they are called what they are called."

Burton smiled. "I think it is because it sort of looks like a frog if you use your imagination. It is the weight bearing part of the foot, and helps absorb and cushion shock. It is also the part that soring trainers will purposely bruise at the tip."

Mick pointed to a white line that surrounded the edge of the hoof. "That is the laminae. It is what holds the hoof wall to the foot structure. This is what is inflamed and damaged in laminitis."

"It looks much better now," Dr.Creola added.

"What does it look like with laminitis?" I asked.

"Sometimes you see the laminae have stretched—the white line there widens or even pulls away from the hoof wall. When you see specks of blood, that is a sure sign of laminitis. Imagine if that tissue swells. The hoof is a rigid wall. There is no place for the swelling to expand to, so it causes excruciating pain." I grimaced, and patted sweet, gentle Sheridan's neck.

"This is the heel bulb." Mick pointed to the back of the hoof.

I nodded. "And this part I use the hoof pick to clean...what's that called?"

"The sole. The back part here near the bulb is called the seats of corn. And no, I don't know why it's called that." Mick stood up.

Burton lowered Sheridan's hoof. "Bruising in the seats of corn can cause lameness too. That's the part where Sheridan's abscess developed, probably from objects purposely placed in the pads of the shoe to apply painful pressure."

I felt like crying, thinking of what poor Sheridan had endured. Mick noticed my tell-tale batting of my eyes, and said, "Now you need to come help me clean out Tripper's stall."

I blinked at him. Tripper's stall? Tripper was the stallion who lived by himself in a shed near the goat pen.

"Ok," I said, forgetting all about boo-hooing over Sheridan's past life. "But where is Tripper?"

"Sold," Burton said, clapping the dust from Sheridan's hooves off his pants.

I looked with uncomprehending confusion, from Burton, over to Milly who stood nearby smiling at me.

"You need a stall. We don't need Tripper. Besides, if we need a stallion, Sheridan is a stallion," Burton said. "And a much nicer stallion than Tripper. We'll exchange the stud fee for the stall if you'll agree to it."

I had never had the slightest inclination to hug Burton. However, I flew against him and wrapped my skinny arms around him. I didn't even think about it. It just happened. As soon as I thought about it, a split second later, I sprang away, fiery red splotches shooting across my cheeks. Mick studied his father with interest, as though he had sprouted wings.

Burton returned Mick's gaze briefly, and then turned to Dr. Creola. "We ready to shoe this horse?"

"We're ready. And Vicky, we will see how he handles his new footwear, and if he looks sound, I think you could try a short ride in the round pen later this week."

I gasped, and almost leaped into Dr. Creola's arms next. Instead, I clasped my hands together, and wondered if Bella had been praying especially hard lately.

I didn't know if I could handle all this unfamiliar camaraderie at Burton's Farm. Fortunately, it was almost feeding time, and there were mountains of chores left to do. Milly came to the rescue of the dangerous swirling emotions, and reminded us that if we wanted to clean the stall, we needed to get right to it since we had only about a half hour before we needed to hay the horses.

Mick and I both grabbed a pitchfork and walked to the shed side by side.

"My dad must be getting senile," he said.

I laughed. "Why?"

"He's never been nice before."

"Neither had you," I said.

"I'm still not nice. Don't start spreading lies."

"You helped me a lot with Sheridan. I never thanked you. But I am really grateful. Really. I mean that."

I never told anyone how much I appreciated them. I often wanted to, but somehow my embarrassment always took over and I never said what I wanted to, what I knew I should. Maybe turning fifteen was a cross-roads into maturity.

I fully expected the retort I knew would come. It always did, but maybe it was wrong of me to withhold doing the right thing because others did not respond the way they should. So I stood tall, braving the expected taunt, knowing it would be a doozy.

"You're welcome," Mick said.

I was right. It *was* a doozy!

Chapter Thirteen

Mick and Bella were the trail guides the next day, and I had a rare hour of no duties. I'd finished my work with Trinity, milked both Cindy the goat and Matilda the cow, and turned Sheridan out into the round pen.

He saw Gidget in the distance and trotted up and down the pen fence, neighing. This was the first time I had seen him trot since his injury. Without his heavy shoes, and painful chains, his gait was almost normal again.

I couldn't imagine why anyone would have tampered with the natural beauty of his gait. His legs certainly didn't snap up as quickly or as high as the champion gaited show horses I'd seen on television, but he had a beautiful natural high step. With his arched neck, and tail held high and streaming behind him, he was the most beautiful horse I had ever seen.

By the way, when I mentioned the beautiful arched tail to Dr. Creola, he shared a story that I would much rather have never heard. You've likely seen those gorgeous show horses with the tails that go straight up from their rumps, and then the long silky hairs cascade down from that gorgeous arch, right? Contrary to what this gullible, deluded little teenager believed, those tails don't do that naturally.

The tendons at the base of the tail are surgically cut, and as the horse heals, the tail is set in a harness that holds the tail up. Show horses wear that harness *always*, until they are retired from showing. If that little piece of cruelty for vanity and extra points at a show doesn't make you want to revoke your membership in the human species, I don't know what will.

Anyway, after sharing that cheery piece of human depravity, Dr. Creola told me that at this point, if Sheridan started trotting or even cantering, I didn't need to worry. He was off all pain medication, the x-rays showed no problem with the coffin bone, and he would not likely do more than he should do in the confines of the round pen. He told me that I could try riding him the very next day.

But for now, I raced out to the pasture with Gidget's hackamore. With Milly's permission, I was going to explore some of the state forest trails that I'd never been on. She had told me not to go more than a half hour out so she would know if I wasn't back in an hour to send out the search and rescue cavalry.

"We'll be careful," I promised her.

Gidget must have sensed we had a special treat. She cantered to me as soon as I catapulted out the back door of the barn. I wasn't sure she was going to stop, she came rocketing over so fast, and then slammed to a stop before trampling me.

She buried her head in my stomach, rubbing her forehead against me. I bridled her quickly and led her through the barn.

"I'm going now!" I called to Milly who was cleaning a muddy saddle pad.

She waved, and told me to be careful.

I leaped onto Gidget's back, went through my usual imitation of a beached whale, and pulled myself upright. Gidget was already prancing by the time I'd gathered the reins. She was as full of hope and energy as me.

I had to rein her in along the Narroway Highway trail section. Milly never liked us to go fast along that section, since she said there were too many crazy things a horse could react to with the busy road nearby.

As soon as I cleared that section, I leaned forward and nudged her sides. She broke into a canter instantly. We stayed on the familiar trail through the trotting section and then veered to the right at the top of the hill. It was the same direction we had seen the motorbike come from on the trail ride a couple of weeks before.

The path led across the open field and then dipped again into a forested area. I slowed her to a walk as we entered the dense foliage. It was ten degrees cooler in the dark green shade. Sounds from the highway were now distant and muffled. It felt like we had entered another world.

There were stands of pine trees all along the path, so the forest floor was lined with a spongy layer of reddish needles. The soft surface absorbed all sound from Gidget's hoof strikes. The strong scent of pine permeated the air around me. Threads of sunlight laced through breaks in the thickly needled boughs.

We moved almost stealthily though the twisted path, so the girl sitting on a rock in front of us didn't even hear us until we were almost upon her. Her red hair was lit by a sunbeam. She spun around when Gidget snorted.

For a moment, I thought she was going to run away, but then she settled back down and sneered.

"Oh. You."

"Hi Fiora."

"Was it you who sic'd Social Service on me?"

I didn't answer.

"It's ok. I suppose you thought you were doing me a favor."

"Where did you hide? Are you staying with someone?"

"I don't think you need to know that."

"What will you do in the winter?" I asked.

"That's my problem."

I shrugged. Gidget pranced a little, nervous in Fiora's presence.

"How's Sheridan?" she asked.

"Better."

"He's lucky."

I nodded. "Listen, Mr. Temple, the man who wants to help you…he's a great guy. He won't let you be hurt."

"I'm not going into the foster care system again," she said.

Again?

"Been there, done that. I can make it on my own."

Until frostbite snapped at all her (overly) exposed parts. How could someone be so deluded? She could no more survive an Illinois winter outdoors than an iceberg in Miami.

"We asked inspectors to show up at the Dupage show. We sent them pictures, and a statement from the vet who worked with Sheridan."

That got her attention. She actually smiled, a real smile. Not the seductive smirk of a trollop. "That could help. I might have to show up myself just to see that ##$#%%^&** nailed."

"I don't know if it will nail him or not. None of it proves he sored the horse he will be showing."

She nodded.

I stroked Gidget's neck. "Did you ever think it was okay? I mean you grew up with a dad who uses soring, right?"

She surprisingly, did not scratch my eyes out. Instead she nodded. "When I was little, and stupid, and believed that parents are good and do the right thing, of course I thought that winning horse shows was all that mattered and if what they did won horse shows, it was good. They hid a lot of the abuse from me, of course. They were evil but not stupid. They come from a completely wacky, different mind-set, the sorers. Horses are commodities to them, no more deserving of humane treatment than a box of Cheerios. If earning their wages depends on abusing horses, then so be it.

"I hit the age where I began to see what was really going on, and how much the horses were suffering. I saw them put several beautiful horses down because they foundered so badly they wouldn't show anymore. Believe me, they didn't care if they foundered in the end as long as they were still winning ribbons. That's when I ran away from home the first time and Social Services decided I was a delinquent."

I could see why Social Services came to that conclusion. She wasn't helping her case by dressing like the whore of Babylon.

"For a while, they sent me back home, and we had therapy. I guess they hoped I would decide that purposely laming horses for a blue ribbon was *not* a good reason to want to stab your father. I confronted him, and told him he was as bad as Hitler. As you can imagine, that didn't go over well. He kicked me out, and I have been on my own ever since."

Gidget stamped her hooves, hoping to dissuade the ever-present flies, who I realized I no longer hated. I looked at Fiora with new respect. I wasn't sure I would have the courage to give up the wealth and comfort of my successful parent's home to live by my conscience. I still didn't know what had happened to her mother, but decided that could wait.

"If I promise Mr. Temple won't call Social Services, can I bring him here to talk with you? Maybe he can help."

She sat solemnly gazing at her long legs, stretched out across the rock. She stroked the back of slender fingers, her fiery hair falling across her cheek. I didn't think she had heard me. Finally she looked up. "Okay. But you come with him. Alone. I will be here tomorrow. Around this time."

Then she stood up and walked away, her hips gyrating in the anatomically impossible circle. I glanced at my watch. My half hour was up. I turned Gidget around, and urged her into a trot.

When we returned, I helped with the night feeding, and then rushed to Bella's house. She was babysitting Maria but told me her father would be back soon. I told her about Fiora, and the whole sad story.

Bella listened, as Bella always did, her face suffused with understanding and compassion. Even before I had finished my story, Mr. Temple returned home. His face was so sorrowful as I recounted Fiora's story that I thought he would cry.

"I will go with you tomorrow," he said, "That poor child."

Chapter Fourteen

We parked at Burton's Farm, and walked along the trail to the pine forest. It was midafternoon, roughly the same time I had seen Fiora the day before. Milly had not asked any questions, being Milly. She trusted me like no one I had ever known before, and I guess she believed that if I could not tell her why Mr. Temple and I had to go out to the pine forest alone, we must have a good reason.

Mick, on the other hand, narrowed his eyes and stared at me with anger. I think he surmised that Fiora was involved in one way or another, and figured I was betraying her.

When we reached the pine forest, Fiora was nowhere in sight. Mr. Temple sat on the very rock Fiora had been sitting on and checked his watch. "We can wait," he said.

We waited an hour. No Fiora.

"I'm sorry," I said.

"It's not your fault," Mr. Temple told me, "You did your best to help her."

He stood up, reluctantly, and glanced into the deep, dark recesses of the forest. There was no sound, and no movement, save the shifting of the pine boughs in the breeze.

As we headed back towards the farm, I told Mr. Temple that I was growing more frightened the more I learned. I had never come up against a mind-set that perceived right so completely differently from me. It would never have occurred to me that someone who was of the same species as me, *homo sapiens*, (Mick would want that clarified,) would think that unbearable pain to an innocent creature could be justified if the perpetrator made money from it.

"It is the danger of a relativistic world view," he said.

I had no idea what that meant.

"You believe, as I do, that there is an absolute standard of decency, and that there is a standard bearer. There is an absolute right and wrong, and your moral compass clearly delineates when the line is crossed."

The sun dipped lower in the sky as we walked back to the farm. I was not really following what Mr. Temple was saying but I was proud that he thought I might be.

"Where do you think that standard comes from? If it is from each person, or each society, then it shifts. Right and wrong changes depending on who is in authority. So the 'plantation morality' that said slavery was right, could also condone that slaves, like animals, were property, and could be used in any way that those in control needed or desired.

"But those of us who believe there is an absolute standard, believe that there is right and wrong that is uncompromising, and unwavering regardless of situation. It is ultimately based upon a moral authority who sets the standard and is unchanging. Right will always be right, in all circumstances. God has written that moral code upon our hearts, and when it is violated, we know at the core of our being it has been violated."

I didn't understand everything Mr. Temple said, but somehow it resonated deep inside me. We had emerged from the pine forest, and were just starting down the trail where the trail horses always trotted when a voice called out, "Wait."

We turned, and saw Fiora, at the edge of the forest, her red hair dancing like fire in the blazing sun. Mr. Temple smiled at her, and said, "Hello, Fiora."

She looked like a wild animal. I sensed she was frightened, but she was also alone and no longer wanted to be alone. I sure could identify with that.

Mr. Temple asked her if she would come home with us. Bella and I would be there too, he assured her. He wanted to feed her dinner and talk with her.

"You don't have to stay if you don't want to and I won't force you to do anything. I just want you to know that if you are willing, we want you to be safe in our home tonight."

Fiora didn't answer at first, looking at me and then at him. I nodded, and told her, "It will be okay. You can trust Mr. Temple."

She shook her red hair that tumbled in tangled clumps across her shoulders. It was like a lion's wild mane. "Okay."

The three of us returned to his car. Mick was loading the flat bed with hay when we walked into the barn yard. He watched silently as Fiora and I got in the front seat, and Mr. Temple slid in the driver's door. (Just for the record, wherever Fiora had been shacking up, it didn't have a bathtub or soap.)

Bella had been cooking, and the house smelled like love, mixed with bacon. (Anything with bacon is divine in my book.) Fiora apparently agreed. She paused and sniffed the air. Maria came dashing over, having heard her father's car rumble up the driveway. She slid to a stop catching her first eyeful of Fiora.

"Where's the rest of your clothes?" she asked.

"Maria." Mr. Temple's soft admonition was registered immediately, and Maria said, "How do you do?" She could not stop gawking however.

Bella appeared from the kitchen, bringing with her extra supercharged bacon molecules.

"Hi Fiora," she said, "I hope you like bacon-wrapped chicken."

"I like bacon-wrapped cardboard," Fiora answered.

"Yeah," Bella agreed, "Bacon makes any cook a Julia Child."

"Will you stay for dinner?" Mr. Temple asked, turning to me.

"I can't," I said. Honestly, I probably could have, but there is only so much a shy, socially backwards girl can be expected to do in one day. Besides, I knew I was leaving Fiora in capable hands.

Fiora looked at me. I hoped she didn't know how uncomfortable I was around her. I was socially inept, but I wasn't cruel.

"Thanks...for everything," she said. I know it cost her everything she had in her to say that to me. Bella watched my face, like she knew what was going on in my heart.

"Maybe I can stay. Let me call my mom."

Mom was happy to let me hang out with the Temples for the night. I knew she would be. The hesitation had been all mine.

The bacon-wrapped chicken was totally awesome. I wondered how Bella learned to cook like that. It had not ever occurred to me that she probably *had* to learn to cook, as the elder female in the home. Her dad worked all day. She was in charge of dinner preparations. If I were in charge at our house, we would have my specialty: Lucky Charms with milk.

As we sat down, Fiora looked around.

"Will Mrs. Temple be here?" she asked.

I looked down, wishing I could escape under the table. But I needn't have worried. Maria instantly filled the silence, "She's always with us, but not here. She's with Jesus."

Fiora faced Maria. "So is my mom."

"What happened to her?" Maria asked.

146

"Maria!" Bella cried.

"It's okay," Fiora said. "She died trying to save a horse."

I dropped my fork. It clattered to the floor. I bent over to pick it up, wishing I could hang out under the table forever.

"We used to have horses," Fiora said. "Dad was just getting into training and Mom had grown up on a horse farm in Tennessee. They bred Tennessee Walking Horses, and showed them. They had some champions. This was back in the days before the soring and *big lick* horses. Then the public kind of lost interest in the breed, and there was a big slump for the breeders and trainers. Mom's family lost a boatload of money. Some trainers started showing up at shows with *big lick* horses, after discovering how to use chemicals to burn and make them step higher in response to the pain. The audience loved them, *big lick* horses started winning, and soring was here to stay."

I knew a little of this from my research with Miss Scruggs. Fiora ate a mouthful of the bacon-wrapped chicken, and pure ecstasy softened her features for a moment. Swallowing, she continued her story.

"So Mom's folks started soring. Mom met Dad, who was a new trainer then. He was still on the fence about soring, and so was Mom. They got married, and their wedding gift was a Tennessee Walker from my grandparents. The horse was young, but really promising. He already had a great gait. He never won, though, cause he couldn't compete with the *big lick* horses. He came in second a lot. Over the years, Dad decided soring was the only way to increase the horse's chances. I was born, and I remember them fighting a lot about soring, though I didn't understand much of it. When I was eight, I was in the barn brushing my horse. I watched my Mom step in the way when she saw Dad beating a horse to get him to stand still while wrapping chemicals into his painful feet. The horse reared, and bashed in Mom's skull."

Even the bacon couldn't entice me to eat another bite.

"You saw that happen?" Bella asked, her face awash with pity.

Fiora nodded. Unlike us, she continued polishing her plate. Maria reached over and patted Fiora's hand. Tiny droplets appeared at the edge of Fiora's eyes. She was not as hardened as I'd thought.

"Your mom was brave," Mr. Temple said.

"And my dad decided to get rid of all the horses after that. But he had a reputation as a trainer, and he became even crueler. The worse he abused the horses, the more they won. And the more I hated him."

She had finished the chicken by now, and pushed her plate away. "That was good. Thank you."

Bella nodded. Mr. Temple sighed deeply. "Fiora, I know you have asked us not to contact the authorities, and we will respect that. Do you think your father worries if you are safe?"

"No. He's the one that booted me."

"If we applied to serve as your foster family, would you be willing to stay?" he asked.

Fiora blinked in surprise. "I'm trouble. You don't know what you are asking."

Bella said nothing. I was incredulous. Never in a billion years would I want the sudden addition of the brazen Fiora as my sister. Sure I felt sorry for her, but charity had its limits.

Not with Mr. Temple though. Or Bella. To my shock, Bella took a deep breath, and said, "We would like you to stay. At least for a while. Just think on it."

Maria said, "Bella has shirts you can borrow."

Mr. Temple was about to chastise Maria again, but then Fiora started laughing. She laughed so hard, that I thought she maybe was hysterical. I was right. She kept laughing till she laid her head on the table, and started crying. Bella put her arm around her, patting her back.

I glanced at the wall clock.

"I gotta get home," I said. "Thanks for dinner." I know. Go ahead and point fingers. I was, and ever would be, a social coward. Mr. Temple smiled weakly, and nodded. I think he understood.

I ran all the way home. Our family had its share of problems. All families do. I mean I fought at every possible moment with my older sister, and my parents squabbled now and then, and my brother got mad and put a fist through the bathroom door once. But never had I doubted the essential goodness of my parents. I'd probably dress like a hooker too if I had the same genes as someone who hurt horses on purpose. That kind of DNA has got to mess with your mind.

The next day was a big one. I had the green light to ride Sheridan in the round pen. I knew Bella would update me on what had happened with Fiora one way or another, so I put that whole sorry mess out of my head.

When I got to the farm, Mick instantly accosted me. He had *not* gotten the whole sorry mess of Fiora out of his head.

"Where were you taking Fiora?" he asked.

"To dinner with Bella."

"She agreed to that?" He was not buying it.

"I don't want to talk about Fiora," I said, "I'm going to ride Sheridan now."

He followed me. Sheridan was not lying down. That was a great sign. He nickered and plopped his head over my shoulder. I fed him from my carrot stash in my pocket.

"What bridle should I use?" I asked Milly.

"They probably used a long shanked, high leverage bridle. We are going to avoid that, though it is what he is used to."

She rummaged in the tack room and came back with a bridle I had never used. She told me it was for English riding, which I had never done.

In some ways, English was easier than Western riding. The reins are held in two hands and you pull on the rein on the side you want him to turn to. In Western riding, the only kind I'd ever done, the reins are used to guide by 'neck reining.' The reins are held in one hand, and the horse is trained to turn as the reins flop together over his neck in the direction you want him to go.

"You think I will be able to figure this out?" I asked.

"Doubtful," mumbled Mick at the same time Milly said, "Yes."

When I went to bridle him, the normally sweet and gentle Sheridan back-stepped, and shrieked. That was completely unexpected. Milly shook her head sadly.

"That's the problem with abused horses," she said. "Often, the abuse causes mental issues. He seemed so gentle and willing, I'd hoped he'd be okay."

I backed to the door immediately, lowering the bridle. He looked at me warily, but was quiet, scrunched in his corner.

"Just put the bridle down and pet him," Mick said. "Leave the bridle hanging on the door."

I glanced at Milly. She nodded. So I approached him slowly, holding a carrot in my palm.

He nibbled it, without any more shrieking or sidling away.

"This is where the trainer probably beat him to make him stand still," Mick said.

I wondered how Mick knew this. As far as I knew, he had never seen or worked with Tennessee Walking Horses, let alone abused ones. Could he possibly have been reading about them?

Sheridan ate the carrot, but never took his eyes off the bridle. He clearly regarded it as an enemy.

"He's connecting the bridle with the pain in the show ring," Milly said.

"How about if I just ride him the way I ride Gidget? With the bridle and a lead rope?"

"He isn't trained to neck rein," she said.

"I could use two leads."

"Vicky, I know you mean well, and you have done remarkably well with Gidget. However, an abused horse is unpredictable. I was hoping he would respond better to the bridle. Seeing how he reacted, I would be worried about you riding him."

"How about me?" Mick asked. "What if I try it first? No offense to Vicky, but I am a better rider."

I was ready to shout *no way.* Not to the statement that he was a better rider. That was irrefutably true. However, no way did I want him to ride Sheridan. I remembered how Mick had spurred my old horse, Joe, so cruelly, sawed on his tender mouth with the reins, and run him into a frantic lather.

Mick looked at me and before I could speak said, "I promise you I will be gentle. I understand this horse has been hurt enough for a lifetime."

Milly examined Mick's face, as though trying to see the ulterior motive. She often excused his behavior, but no doubt she knew what he was capable of.

"The halter idea might work. I would be comfortable with Mick on him the first time, if you will agree to that Vicky. If he is all right with Mick, you could try."

Mick turned to me, eyes pleading.

"Remember, I helped you clean his new stall...."

That was true. And I could count the number of insults on one hand in that half hour as we worked together. That was probably a new minimum record.

"If you swear on...a stack of *Bellas* that you won't hurt him. No matter what he does to you."

Mick grinned, and held up his right hand. "I do."

I haltered Sheridan without incident, and snapped two leads to the halter. Mick followed me as I led him out of the stall. Milly tagged along as well. I am certain Burton would have joined us if he were around, but he was off on a farrier job.

Sheridan had been led to the round pen several times, so this caused no distress. "Remember Mick, just walk him. Dr. Creola said this was just to be minimal exercise at first."

"Yes, worry-wart."

Mick leaned his weight across Sheridan's back. No response other than some ear twitching. I held Sheridan, quietly crooning to him, "It's ok boy, it's ok."

Mick put the two leads on either side of Sheridan's neck, and then in a single graceful bound, settled onto his back. Sheridan's head shot up, but he didn't move. Mick gathered the 'reins.'

"OK, let go," he told me.

I stepped back. Sheridan began walking forward. I almost cried. He snapped his legs up in the exaggerated *big lick* step.

"You don't have to do that," I whispered.

Mick pulled back on the lead ropes to stop him. He halted immediately. Then Mick urged him forward. The hoof snapped up in the air. Mick stopped him again. He sat quietly, petting Sheridan's neck. He squeezed his heels against the horse's side, and Sheridan again strode into the *big lick* walk. This sequence repeated over and over again. I knew what Mick was doing. He was trying to communicate that the high leg was not necessary.

Finally, he hopped off Sheridan.

"Come here, Vicky. You get on. I'm going to lead him."

He held out his hands for my knee, and boosted me on Sheridan's back.

"Just sit there," Mick said. "Don't give any cues to him at all except holding the reins."

Mick started off, leading Sheridan. To both our delight, he walked almost normally. Mick circled the ring twice. We stopped at the gate, and I slid off. I gave Sheridan a palm full of carrots.

"That was a smart idea," I told Mick.

"Maybe I can market it. Sell it as the *anti-big lick* training method. It will probably take as long to train him out of that goofy gait as it took to train him into it."

"I guess you're stuck being my partner again. I don't see how I can do this alone."

"I don't see how you do *anything* alone."

Chapter Fifteen

Bella told me that for now, Fiora was staying with them. Mr. Temple told her at some point, soon, he would have to notify the authorities. Not to mention her father. But for now, he would consider it an extended sleep-over from a friend of his daughter.

Bella told me that the first night, Fiora took a two-hour bath.

"Two hours! Who can soak in a bath two hours? When she came out, she was wrinkled like a raisin, but she smelled a lot better. I had thrown her so-called clothes in the wash, and loaned her my t-shirt and shorts. She told me it was blasphemy calling them shorts. But she put them on. She almost looked like a normal girl."

"So where is she now?"

"Sleeping. She must not have slept much wherever she was before. She has been sleeping almost non-stop since she came."

Bella and I were walking together to the farm. Mr. Temple was working from home, and urged Bella to 'go have fun.'

"Do you know where she was staying?" I asked.

"No. I don't think she was actually sleeping in the forest, but she won't tell us who has been helping her. I think she plans to go back, wherever it was."

We walked in silence, listening to crickets chirping in the tall grass of the vacant field adjoining the farm and the side street that led to Bella's neighborhood.

"What will your father do?"

"I'm not sure," Bella said, "For now, he is waiting on God to direct him."

"Does God do that?"

Bella nodded, smiling at me.

"How?" I asked.

"Different ways. Sometimes He opens doors in unexpected ways."

I suspected she didn't mean literally. If there were real doors in heaven, I would have heard them slamming at least now and then. I still didn't understand how God, completely invisible and mute, could direct living human beings.

"How do you know it is God who opened the door?" I asked finally.

"Sometimes you don't. Sometimes you walk through and find out."

This whole God thing sounded like a massive game of dice. There was nothing definitive in how He worked that I could discern.

"It's just two weeks till the Dupage show," Bella said, "Do we know if the inspectors will be there?"

"No," I said, "and if they do come, we don't know if they will be able to find anything. You would not believe what sorers do to avoid detection. I just found out that some vets actually prescribe a drug that masks the trace of the pain killers sorers use on the horses to pass inspection at the shows. If the vets are being bribed to help the sorers, I don't know what hope there is in catching them."

"I guess we just pray and wait and see," she said. But she looked troubled. Even people of endless faith like Bella had to get down looking at how often evil people got away with so much wrong-doing. For example, Fiora's father.

Much as I didn't love Fiora, I loved her father even less. How could a father do what he was doing to his own daughter? Where was God in that? You would think He would notice, particularly if He was in the business of numbering all our hairs, which according to Bella, He was. His time might be better spent paying attention to some of the obvious sin going on, like soring, rather than counting hair.

"What are you doing with Sheridan today?" Bella asked.

"Mick says we do more of the same. I am a little surprised at how patient he is being. He's acting almost like someone who cares."

Bella grinned at me, as her fingers tickled across a stand of Queen Anne's Lace. They were a weed, but I loved their fragile white flowers that did indeed look like lace.

"I think he feels bad for Sheridan. Maybe he is starting to reevaluate some things in his life."

"He doesn't call me names nearly as often," I said.

"Maybe he is looking at cruelty with new eyes."

"Maybe. He does seem to really want to help. I didn't even ask him. He volunteered."

We rounded the corner into the barn yard. Peeper and Tara were sitting on a hay bale together, their heels kicking its side in tandem.

"Yay!" Tara said, jumping off the bale. "Can we work with Trinity?"

She ran to me and threw her arms around my waist. I hugged her back briefly. "Yep. We'll do that first thing!"

As we walked past Sheridan's stall on the way out to the pasture, he nickered to me. We both stopped and stroked his nose. While I was feeding him carrots, Milly passed by and asked if Bella and I could lead the trail due out in an hour.

"I'll start brushing and tacking the horses," Bella said.

I nodded. Tara and I hurried out the back door.

"What are we doing today?" Tara asked. Gidget and Trinity stood together, and both watched us with interest as we approached.

"How about if I teach you how to have Trinity trot on the lunge line today?"

"Yay!"

Tara was only eight-years-old now, but she was eager to learn, and loved Trinity. She was becoming a very good rider, since her pony Nipper lived in a small field adjoining her house. She rode regularly and it showed.

She loved the lessons with me, and what was even more surprising, I didn't mind teaching her. I guess I was reevaluating some things just like Mick was.

Nothing worth reporting happened during our lesson. Trinity knew all the voice commands by now, and she was super smart. I showed Tara how to hold the lunge line, and position her body and the long whip to show Trinity she wanted her to change direction. The hour flew by. Leaving Tara with a brush and some treats, I led Gidget into the barn for the trail ride.

Gidget paused as we passed Sheridan's stall and touched noses with him. He nibbled at her face. Little horse kisses.

"When you finish the trail ride," Mick called from the tack room, "We're going to trot Sheridan today."

I had never been on a gaited horse trotting. I had read that the trot was smooth and comfortable. Gidget's trot was jarring. It would be fun to ride a rocking trot that was easy to sit.

The trail ride for that day was a small group with only five riders. Bella told me she thought this should be her last ride on

Skippy. "I think it's time I start riding one of the bigger horses," she said. It really was a day of reevaluating!

No catastrophes, or even minor mishaps, marred the trail ride. Every rider was happy, and no one was injured or endured any problem other than one horse who wouldn't stop gobbling tree leaves as he passed by them.

Afterwards, Bella helped untack the horses, and said she had to get back home. She hated leaving her dad alone too long with the responsibility of both Maria and Fiora.

"And I promised Fiora I would teach her how to make brownies," she said, waving goodbye to me. I had a hard time framing that picture in my mind. *Susie Homemaker* did not come to mind easily when considering Fiora.

"Ready?" Mick appeared at my side.

I haltered Sheridan, and led him out to the ring. We had not attempted to bridle him again after the first day. He responded well to the halter with lead rope reins. Thus far, every time Mick tried to ride him alone, he still high stepped with his weight shifted over his rear legs. He looked like a praying mantis.

We worried at first that his front hooves still hurt, but Dr. Creola assured us that was not likely. The poor horse just didn't know he didn't need to do that anymore. It wouldn't have been a major concern, except that his whole demeanor changed as soon as Mick tried riding him in the ring. His eyes widened with a pained, fearful expression. He breathed heavily, as though he were reliving the torment of his soring days.

"It's like post-traumatic stress disorder," Dr. Creola said after watching him one day. He even measured his pulse and said poor Sheridan's heart was racing. The riding was bringing back unhappy memories.

However, as long as Mick led him, even when I was riding him, his response was less dramatic, less stressed. Then the moment Mick got on him without someone else leading him, the frightened pained look returned, along with the *big lick* stepping. I was worried he would never get over his trauma from the soring.

"Oh ye of little head," Mick said. "It will just take time. It's not like you to bail on a horse."

"I'm not bailing. I just feel so bad for him."

"Pity won't help him," Mick said, "But teaching him we won't hurt him will. It just might take a while."

Then Mick laughed. "Have you noticed it's like we've exchanged brains lately?"

I had. Scary thought.

"What if I ride him after you lead us around the ring? Maybe he'll be calmer. Should we try?"

Mick nodded. Sheridan was fine as Mick led him at a trot around the ring. Then Mick let go and stepped back. As soon as Mick dropped the lead rope, Sheridan's eyes grew wild, his exaggerated *big lick* steps took over, and his mouth foamed.

"Whoa, boy, hooooe." I pulled the reins, leaning back. Sadly, something must have snapped in his tortured brain. My guess is a flashback to the abuse took over his present reality.

He screamed out as though I'd hurt him, though I knew I hadn't. Then he reared. He reared so suddenly and so violently, that I knew he was about to topple over backwards.

"Get off! Get off!!!" Mick shouted.

For the record, that is easier said than done. I know Bella would have said that what happened next proved the existence of God. As Sheridan came crashing down on his back, I slid off to the side just in the nick of time. I rolled away from his flailing hooves, unhurt.

Mick ignored me, who he assessed as undamaged, and raced to Sheridan. As suddenly as the demonic possession had appeared, it now vanished. Sheridan stood up slowly as Mick held the lead rope.

Mick didn't have to tell me this was bad news.

"If we tell Mom, she won't let us near him."

I pursed my lips. I hated to withhold information from Milly, but I knew Mick was right. She was way too worried about us not dying, and would not let us near Sheridan if she knew how close I'd come to being pancaked. Sheridan's sudden shift to psychotic had been terrifying. I knew my limitations well enough to know I hadn't a prayer of helping this horse without Mick's assistance. I was not even close to being a good enough rider to deal with this.

"What do we do now?"

Gidget had appeared at the side fence, nearest the ring, and now whinnied to me. She might have been calling to Sheridan. She was a perceptive horse. I bet she knew he was distressed. Sheridan neighed in response and started tugging Mick towards the gate.

"Maybe he needs the comfort of a woman," Mick said, winking at me. He opened the gate and led Sheridan to the fence. The two horses nuzzled each other. Gidget nibbled at his ears as he bowed his head. It looked like she was telling him a secret.

"What do you think happened to him in there?" I asked, nodding towards the ring.

"I think he remembered what they did to him."

"They never ride Tennessee Walking show horses outside a show ring," I said.

He smirked at me. "You know that from your countless years owning and showing Walkers?"

"No, I read. They don't want to take a chance with the sored feet on uneven surfaces so they work them only in the ring. I bet he has no bad memories being ridden on a trail."

Mick gazed at me, wonderment creeping across his smile.

"That is not a half- ##$#%%^&** idea, mini-skullion."

Mini-skullion? That was a new one.

"And he likes Gidget," I said. "What if we rode together on the trail? Just a short ways." The more I considered my idea, the better it sounded.

"You'd have to ride Gidget," Mick said, "You can't ride Sheridan. It's too dangerous, and you are too terrible."

"That was my plan," I said, brushing off the insult. He was correct, though as always, he ignored the little conversational aid known as *tact*.

"Go ahead. Get Gidget. I will meet you at the trail head. Sneak by Mom."

I hurried out to the pasture, grabbing the hackamore on my way past the tack room. Milly was there, putting the trail horse saddles away for the day.

"How was Sheridan in the ring?"

"We thought he would enjoy a brief walk on the trail, if that's ok. I would ride Gidget beside Mick. Is that all right?"

I hoped she didn't notice I'd hedged her question.

"Don't go far," she said.

I scurried off before she sniffed a whiff of guilt accumulating in the air around me.

Gidget was overjoyed to see me. She nuzzled me rigorously, almost knocking me over. I think she was beginning to notice that she was always waiting her turn with me. I wondered if she minded.

I flopped onto her back, and reined her in Mick's direction. The flaw in our plan suddenly occurred to me.

"What if he freaks out again?" I asked. "It might be dangerous right next to the highway."

"I'll jump off and stop him, but I don't think he will. He seems calm right now."

Sheridan touched noses to greet Gidget. Mick mounted easily, with the effortless swing of his leg that I could never come close to replicating.

I clucked to Gidget, squeezing my calves against her sides, and we started side by side with Sheridan down the trail. Sheridan still picked his legs up higher than when being led, but he didn't seem overly stressed.

His walk was faster than Gidget's. High stepping aside, something else about his leg movements struck me as unusual. I didn't know enough about normal gaits to detect what was different.

"He walks funny."

"He's got a natural flat walk," Mick said.

"What do you mean?"

"See how the front and back leg on the same side move together? But listen to the rhythm."

I couldn't figure out what Mick wanted me to notice.

"The hooves all hit at a slightly different moment. It feels like gliding, and it's why this breed was so desired in the first place."

I could see now what Mick meant. He seemed to be gliding slightly back and forth on Sheridan's back rather than bouncing gently, like I did, even at a walk.

"They are most famous for their running walk," Mick told me.

"That's like jumbo shrimp. What do you mean by running walk?"

"Watch."

Mick squeezed his legs against Sheridan's sides, and his pace instantly accelerated. He wasn't trotting, but he was moving at least as fast as Gidget could trot. In fact, to keep up with him, I had to prod Gidget to trot.

"Man, it's like riding butter!" Mick exclaimed.

Sheridan's head bobbed noticeably with each step. I asked Mick if that was okay. I was worried it meant his feet still hurt.

"No, it's normal," Mick said. "I think he's having fun."

I agreed. I was bouncing around like a tennis ball in a washing machine. Mick was so enthralled with the effortless gait of Sheridan that he seemed to have forgotten me, and thus I escaped the usual insult.

Despite my warnings to not go fast or far, Mick urged Sheridan into a canter. I would have screamed at him, except Sheridan looked so comfortable and calm that I decided it was best to go with the flow. Mick had the good sense to pull up at the top of the small hill. Sheridan responded immediately.

That was a surprise given the lack of a bit in our makeshift bridle. Milly told me the bridle he was accustomed to had a long shank and curb bit which worked on the principle of a lever. She said for every pound of pressure on the reins, such a bridle produced three pounds of pressure on the chin groove and four pounds of pressure on the horse's mouth. *Good golly* that creeped me out. I wouldn't want anyone pressuring *my* mouth that way!

"Man, this is the smoothest horse I've ever ridden." Mick was glowing with enthusiasm, as Sheridan pranced beneath him, and then shook his gorgeous mane.

I was jealous. My brain felt a little rattled by Gidget's choppy trot, though our brief canter had been glorious. However, I couldn't get too upset. He was *my* horse, after all, though as of yet I had never successfully ridden him without being led.

"We probably should turn around," I cautioned.

Mick scowled, and the old reckless look I knew so well threatened to return. However, it only flashed for a moment, and he nodded. The horses walked side by side.

"That was a good idea you had, about trying him on the trail," Mick said, as we clattered onto the barn yard gravel driveway. "I may have to reconsider entering you in the Shriveled Brain contest."

Chapter Sixteen

Unfortunately, our success on the trail did not translate to improvement in the riding ring as we had hoped. The next day, we brought Sheridan and Gidget to the ring, thinking that now Sheridan would trust us, understanding that we could ride him and not hurt him. The success on the trail ride had been so spectacular, that we were convinced we had pierced the bubble of fear soring had created.

"How about if you just walk Gidget beside us and I ride Sheridan?" I suggested. I was dying to get on him, and ride that smooth running walk.

"That would indicate you are reverting to cranio-nimbicile again. By the way that species is extinct…with good reason."

"Look at him, Mick. He is calm, and smooching with Gidget."

He was too. He was nibbling her cheek.

"He was calm right before he reared and almost turned you into a dork-cake too."

"He's *my* horse," I said, pouting.

"That's true. And if he kills you, my parents will be sued. If he kills me, they will just collect my life insurance. Let me ride him first, and then we'll see."

I handed him the 'reins'. The reins were still the lead ropes. We saw no good reason to try a real bridle since he was doing so well with the halter and leads.

Sheridan stood calmly, swishing flies away with his long tail. I couldn't get over what a nice horse he was, especially knowing his history. Except for when he was possessed by memories that would turn anyone into a psycho, he was the most easy going horse I'd ever known.

During my research into soring, I'd read that docility and amiability were common characteristics of the Tennessee Walking Horse. These admirable qualities were the very things that allowed soring trainers to be so cruel to them. That disgusted me. Soring was perpetrated on one of the few breeds so gentle and kind that they put up with it. If I were a horse, I would be headed for the gas chamber on multiple counts of murder if someone tried that torment on me.

Mick sprung atop Sheridan with his typical effortless fluidity. I scrambled, and groaned, and flopped about till I managed to pull my awkward self atop Gidget.

"Poetry in motion," Mick said, watching me.

I clicked to Gidget, squeezing her sides with my heels. "Walk girl."

Sheridan started off beside us, perfectly composed. Then, out of nowhere, his nostrils flared, he squealed, and he shot into the air in a frantic rear. Gidget startled, and shied, leaping out of hoof strike range. I was unprepared and flew off her back, slamming to the ground in a tangled heap.

Mick, being a superior rider (by a universe or two) managed to stay on, and instinctively dug his heels in, spurring Sheridan forward. The poor horse's eyes were wild, as he dashed forward. Gidget was now racing around the ring, with Sheridan on her tail. I rolled out of the way, scrambled to my feet, and hurtled over the fence before the crazy horses thundered by again.

Mick did not fight Sheridan. I would have been frantically pulling on the makeshift reins, shouting stop in every language I knew (which was exactly one).

Not Mick. He leaned forward and low over Sheridan's withers, face close to his neck. He kept the 'reins' short, but not pulling on Sheridan's head at all. He looked like he was on a race horse. I watched from the safety of the other side of the fence in amazement.

Gidget was no help in the situation. Her spook-switch was flipped fully on, and clearly nothing was registering but the need to run. She stampeded by me, tail streaming behind her, breath spurting from her dilated nostrils.

Sheridan was close behind, with much the same wild-eyed terror. Mick, on the other hand, looked like he was having fun. If I hadn't been so worried about what was happening to Sheridan's hooves, I would have been utterly captivated by admiration for Mick. His arms were loose and relaxed, moving in rhythm with the rise and fall of Sheridan's head. His knees were high, and lower legs tucked tight under him, like a jockey. His legs were still, as they clamped Sheridan's side. Mick was a superb rider. No one could deny that.

It felt like an hour before the frenzied horses finally slowed to a canter, which fizzled to a trot, and at last, a gasping walk. Their chests heaved as they sucked in air.

Sheridan was stepping normally, without the exaggerated *big lick* gait. I was happy to see that, at least. Another good thing: he didn't appear to be limping. If anything would have compromised all the healing in his feet, that would have. Gidget stopped by the gate, hanging her head as she breathed in huge gasps of air.

However, Mick nudged Sheridan forward, urging him to continue walking around the ring. He petted his neck, saying something in a low, soothing voice. Sheridan's ears flicked back and forth listening.

Taking that as a cue, I slipped back in the ring and took a hold of Gidget's reins. On foot, I led Gidget behind Sheridan. After that wild dash, a cool-down session was a good idea. After two laps around the ring, at a walk, Mick told me to mount Gidget.

"Why?" I asked.

"Because horses are beasts of burden," he said. "Do you argue every time your parents tell you to stop playing in the middle of the road?"

I clambered up on Gidget, and fell in behind him again.

"We're gonna trot," Mick said, without turning. "I think it will be fine now."

Sheridan responded quickly to Mick's body cues, with the beautiful running walk. His hooves did not snap up as they had earlier. It was really quite miraculous. Mick's instincts were right on the money.

Gidget was perfect, too. She trotted calmly behind Sheridan. I guess all the heebie-jeebies had been whisked out of them both on their panic-stricken rout. This was the glorious moment that Milly came to check on us.

She stood at the gate watching. We both came to a controlled stop in front of her. "Well now. They look stunning. No problem, huh?"

"Nope. Not a bit," Mick said, sliding off Sheridan's back. He glanced back at me and winked. *Winked!* I know. The end-times must be due any second.

I was dying to get on Sheridan now, thinking surely he would be calm with me at this point. However, it would have been foolish to do so with Milly watching. If he went ballistic again, the ruse would be exposed.

"Vicky, if you are up to it, there's a group that just called for a trail ride in half an hour. Would you want to lead it on Gidget?"

"Sure," I said.

"Mick, Dr. Creola is here, and as long as you have just finished Sheridan's work-out, he would like to check him over."

We both dismounted, and led our horses, following Milly back into the barn.

"It's good to see Sheridan doing so well," Milly said to me, "I would have expected more problems given how strongly he reacted to the bridle."

Mick flicked his eyes at me, and put a finger quickly to his mouth in his classic *shush your mouth, pea-head* signal. I scowled at him. He needn't have bothered warning me. I knew if Milly had gotten the real low-down on how our training was shaping up, Sheridan would be on his way to the meat-factory.

Dr. Creola asked us how the session had gone. Mick and I looked at each other. It was one thing to bamboozle Milly, but we knew Dr. Creola probably needed to know about the madcap racing.

Fortunately, Milly offered to go catch the trail horses while we talked with Dr. Creola. As she disappeared, I told Dr. Creola about what Sheridan had done. I didn't tell him about rearing and flipping the day before. Full disclosure was not necessary, in my opinion. However, he needed to know about the uncontrolled gallop, in case it had done damage to his hooves.

Dr. Creola didn't freak out, like Milly for sure would have. He was impressed with Mick's intuition in giving Sheridan his head, and letting him run. I hadn't been sure that was a good idea. However, Dr. Creola was very reassuring.

"I am sure his behavior is not unusual for a mistreated horse," Dr. Creola said, "Abuse can cause the animal to react over triggers you may not immediately recognize. But it sounds like he is beginning to understand he can trust you."

"He was fine yesterday on the trail," Mick said. "He didn't show any sign of freaking out. But both times we rode him in the ring he went nuts."

"That makes sense," Dr.Creola said, "It was in the show ring that the most painful moments occurred. It is not surprising riding in the ring would trigger flash-backs of what he endured."

"Will he get over it?" I asked.

"I guess only time will tell."

Dr. Creola bent down and checked all over Sheridan's legs. He poked and prodded, especially in the pastern area just above the hooves. Sheridan didn't react at all. Then Dr.Creola lifted each hoof and poked around, carefully examining each part.

"He looks all right. It would probably not be a bad idea to ice his hooves."

I breathed a sigh of relief.

"I'll do that for you," Mick offered, turning to me, "So you can get ready for your trail and help with the trail horses."

Don't be too impressed by Mick's generosity. This was not a magnanimous gesture. Instead of work, he got to hang out with my horse. However, Sheridan was looking with dreamy eyes at Mick as he stroked his neck. It pained me to admit it, but Sheridan *liked* Mick. Gidget nudged me, reminding me I had full pockets of carrots that had not been offered yet. I rectified that problem, to her delight, then gathered a brush and curry comb to groom her.

"Whatever happened with your call to the Dupage show inspectors?" Dr.Creola asked me.

I told him we didn't know if they would show up. "But they were glad that you had described Sheridan's injuries. They said a lot of vets will not speak up."

"I understand the hesitancy of horse people to let government regulate what they do. I sure don't want a government official who doesn't know a horse's rear from his muzzle deciding what I can and can't do with a horse.

"But in a case like soring, I think to do nothing when you know what is happening to those poor horses....I just couldn't do that."

"Burton was threatened if he said anything," I said, "And Fiora told us that she knew some trainers who speak out against it have had death threats. Are you scared?"

"No. I am not in the TWH industry. They can't hurt me. Most of the animals in my practice are small independent farms like Burton's. The show horse vets tend to specialize in the breed."

"Have you ever worked with a horse like Sheridan before?" I asked.

"Once. That horse didn't make it though. His coffin bone had rotated and he was in chronic, constant pain. The kindest thing to do was put him down. I gave treatment a shot for a couple of weeks, but the pain those horses go through when the bones are damaged is unbearable. I didn't have the heart to put him through any more."

"Why do they get away with it?" I asked.

Dr. Creola shook his head, looking down.

"Maybe this time they won't," I said. I left Gidget tied to the wall, and passed Milly bringing in two of the trail horses.

"I saw Bella on her way over. Maybe she can help as the trail follower," Milly told me, "Though she had a friend with her. Looked a little like that girl that came by once or twice looking to help out. It was hard to tell across the field."

Fiora? When I saw her, I understood why Milly hadn't immediately recognized her. If I hadn't known it was Fiora, I might not have known it was her either when she walked in the barn with Bella. Her wild red hair was tied back in a perky pony tail. She was wearing one of Bella's t-shirts with the incongruous slogan, "Let Go and Let God." The shorts were clearly Bella's too, being about a meter longer than the postage stamp shorts Fiora normally wore.

Mick glanced up when they walked in the barn, and his eyes narrowed. I could tell exactly what he was thinking. *What did you do to her? You ruined her.*

The physical changes were pretty astonishing, but perhaps not as incredible as the fact that she and Bella were laughing companionably. Bella seemed to be finishing some story, laying her *pure as the driven snow* hand on Fiora's forearm. I wondered if she would recoil, or spontaneously combust, but nothing like that happened.

"Hi Fiora," Dr. Creola said, recovering speech before the rest of us.

She smiled at him. "I heard what you did to help Sheridan. I wanted to tell you thank you. I wanted to help him the moment I saw him, but I didn't know what to do."

"Oh, you are most welcome. How do you know Sheridan?"

"He was first trained, if you want to call it that, by my dad. As a yearling. Tortured is a better word to describe it."

I listened in surprise. Fiora's story was growing increasingly enmeshed in mine by the minute, and she was full of new revelations with each encounter.

"As a yearling!" I said. I had no idea the training started that young. "How old is he now?"

"He's only three," she said. "That's probably why he hasn't been ruined yet. You got him out of there fast enough."

"What do they do with yearlings?" Even as I asked, I wasn't sure I wanted to know. My psyche might not be able to withstand the knowledge. However, Bella was always telling me the truth was important to know, because "the truth will set you free."

"They get a 'package' at twelve months." Fiora sneered as she spat out the words.

"A package?"

"Hoof pads specially designed for yearlings. I won't go into all the gory details, but it starts to shape and deform the hoof. The goal is to get the weight forward on the toe bones."

"Why?"

"As the hoof grows, it's trimmed to accommodate the 'package'. The toe bone gets longer, and bears the load of the horse's weight. That causes the colt to learn to snap its hoof up. The idea is to 'stick' the foot to the ground during loading so that when the hoof breaks over, it will "explode" from the ground with large amounts of energy, which causes the *big lick*. If you add weight to the pads, the force is even stronger."

"Sadistic," Dr. Creola said. I suspected he had not known about this practice starting with the young Tennessee Walking Horses. I sure didn't. All my research hadn't uncovered this piece of despicable information.

"You know one of the saddest results? It changes everything in the horse. It is not how the horse is designed to move, so it stresses not only the foot, but the shoulders, the hips, and the spine. It even changes the thing that made the Tennessee Walking Horse famous in the first place, their natural gait. It turns the running walk into a pace. If you look at the newsletters about Tennessee Walking

Horses, one of the most common questions is why the horse won't gait up properly…all it wants to do is pace. That's why."

I knew I was showing my ignorance, a dangerous practice when facing what I knew could be a formidable enemy. But at least in this, we were on the same side, so I asked her. "What's a pace?"

"There's four beats in a normal running walk gait. Pacing is two beats. The front and back hoof on the same side of the horse hit together and move in tandem. That's not how most horses walk or trot."

"Is it bad?" I asked.

"It's not how they are designed," she said. "It's like having you, I don't know, skip everywhere you would normally walk."

"She *does* do that," Mick said. That was not a true statement. I only skipped when I thought no one was watching. And sometimes I cantered. But contrary to what Mick said, those were exceptions, not the rule.

Dr. Creola nodded, listening to Fiora. "She's right. The damage to the horse can be widespread. Many of them end up in the slaughter house after their brief show career. Some have long careers, but none escape physiological damage if they are sored."

"And all the *big licks* are sored," Fiora said with disgust, "Don't let anyone tell you otherwise."

Chapter Seventeen

Dr. Creola was fully invested. The day of the Dupage show arrived, and he promised us we could ride over to the fairgrounds with him. All of us would descend on the unsuspecting sorers and attend the very popular *big lick* class.

Fiora was with us too. Ever since that day in the barn, we were a united front in our desire to punish Bob Mortis.

Bella hedged when I asked the status of Fiora with regards to her legal residence. That was not at all Bella-like, but I think she was torn in two directions. There was the law, which clearly said Fiora should be turned over to Social Services. Then there was the promise that Mr. Temple and Bella had made to Fiora. They would not go back on their promise, so the 'overnight' with a friend was now going on three weeks.

I was surprised Mick wanted to go to the Dupage show, and even more surprised when both Milly and Burton encouraged it. They were losing their two top workers for most of the day, but both insisted we needed to be there.

"Someone has to take a stand," Burton said. He frowned, and darted a look at Milly. She touched his arm gently.

Dr. Creola drove the five of us to the fairgrounds. The class was due to start in an hour. We milled around, looking for signs of the inspectors. None of us, except perhaps Fiora, knew what to look for. However, we found seats, one row back from the arena gate. The five of us settled down with a program.

As luck (*"Not luck. God,"* Bella said) would have it, a duo of Tennessee Walking Horse trainers plopped down in front of us. I knew that because they had shirts with the iconic picture of a silhouette of a TWH in the classic *big lick* pose.

"Don't see any today," one of the trainers said. His voice was low, and hissing, like a snake. "We'll go ahead and unload then."

"Who you showing today?"

A list of names. Five horses.

"Oh ##@#$^^&*! Look there!"

The other trainer pointed, and we saw a man in a white shirt setting up orange cones, outside the show ring. I didn't know what that meant, but the trainers were clearly not happy.

"Gotta go," the first said, his voice snapping the words with venom.

The second swore, under his breath, muttered, "Oh the ##5$$&," and left as well. I leaned over to Mick, "Are those the inspectors?"

"I guess so," Mick said.

Fiora groaned in disgust. "The sorers will just leave if they see them. They'll just scratch from the class. I thought you told them to come afterwards?"

"We asked them to," I said, "But we have no control."

We watched, all disheartened. A horse was being led in a figure eight pattern around the cones. The inspector wasn't even watching. He glanced briefly at the horse, then wrote on the paper on his clipboard.

"That horse is obviously in pain," Dr. Creola said. "See how he doesn't even want to walk, and he is shifting his weight back on his rear legs. Those front hooves hurt."

The inspector bent down, made a brief cursory look at the horse's legs, and waved him on. We saw the trainer give a subtle thumbs up to someone in the small crowd watching the inspection.

"He passed," Fiora spat out. "It's an industry inspector."

"What's that?" asked Bella.

"People in the TWH industry who are hired to self-police their own breed. I see it over and over. They don't even examine or watch the horse, and look away. They pass horses just like that one, obviously sore."

"All of them?" Bella asked, "They can't all be corrupt."

Fiora shrugged.

"Maybe the government inspectors will still come after the class," Bella said.

"They won't. But even if they did," Fiora said, "Bob Mortis is too smart to show a sored horse, unless he's bribed this inspector. Maybe he has."

"I'll pray for that," Bella said, laying her hand on Fiora's leg.

"Look!" I cried.

We all turned to the inspection ring.

"Speaking of the devil!" Mick said, "And I mean that literally."

It was Bob Mortis, leading in a black TWH stallion. The horse didn't walk as obviously in pain as the horse before.

"He probably is shot up with short-term pain killer," Fiora said. "It will wear off in time for the show so his hooves hurt for the *big lick* torture time." She leaned back with a thud, crossing her arms, and glaring at Mortis. If looks could kill, Bob Mortis would be a sunken, rotting corpse.

The inspector again made a quick, cursory look at the horse's pasterns, and nodded to Mortis. He was smiling as he left the inspection area, so we knew he'd passed.

"Scum," Fiora blurted. Then she shot up in her seat and gasped as the next trainer led a horse in.

"That's my dad. The *$$#@#$%%&**!*"

Mr. Heller was a tall handsome man. He did not look like someone possessed by Satan, as I had expected. No one would know by looking at him what power of evil he possessed. For some reason, this shocked me. It seemed to me that someone capable of such cruelty should look like Frankenstein.

He led three different horses through the inspection. All passed.

"That's a crock!" Fiora spat out, "I know for a fact that every horse he shows is sore. All of them."

We watched a total of twelve horses inspected. All except for a light colored horse had the classic *big lick* walk. All but one of them passed inspection.

"He's bribed for sure," Fiora growled. "Every one of those horses has been sored. I bet the dumb loser that got nailed didn't pay the extortion fee."

I was feeling sick to my stomach. I didn't know how I could watch this class. Bella leaned over and whispered, "It will be okay. Maybe your government inspector will still be here."

I was too dispirited to argue. I knew with the limited funds that there was no way the government inspectors would show up if the industry inspectors were assigned to assess the horses. The government inspectors must have decided to focus on the big Celebration show in Shelbyville a couple of weeks out. I didn't blame them, but I was horribly disappointed.

All of us watched the horses file in with varying mixtures of horror and sadness on our faces. The horse Bob Mortis trained was second in the ring. I could hardly stand to see the anguished recoiling of his hooves from the ground. Knowing what I knew, I saw torture with every step. How anyone with a heart could watch these horses and find beauty in the tormented, unnatural movement was beyond my comprehension.

"Those next three are my Dad's horses," Fiora said as the horses who were 6th, 7th, and 8th in line filed in. Those three had the most exaggerated steps of all. Not only did the hooves rise above chest level, but they stretched far out in front before touching the ground again. It was the craziest gait I had ever seen, and yet the crowd erupted in ear-splitting cheers.

Fiora crouched down in her seat in case her father was watching as the horses filed past us. I couldn't bear to watch the ridiculous stride, yet was mesmerized as strongly as repulsed. I could not believe any horse who outweighed humans ten-fold would submit to anything that would so distort their normal movements. The crowd did not share my disgust. The cheers and whistling escalated.

Then Horse #9 entered. The crowd fell silent. The cheering came to a sudden halt. The whistles ended, like a boiling teapot pulled off the heat. It was the one *non-big-lick* horse in the group. The light colored horse walked with a lovely high step, though not an exaggerated one like all the others. The balance between front and hind quarters was even. It didn't look like the poor horse was about to fall on his tail, like all the others. The rider sat tall and proud, not hunched forward like all the *big lick* riders.

As the rider passed our bleacher seats, Fiora stood, and began clapping. All eyes in the arena turned on her, presumably including her father's. Bella slowly rose, and stood beside her, clapping as well. Then Mick, and Dr. Creola, and I all stood. I don't know about anyone else, but tears were streaming down my cheeks.

The rider atop horse #9 ever so imperceptibly turned her eyes toward us, and smiled. We cheered, the sole members of that entire audience applauding the one rider who chose to defy the call of the *big lick* siren.

When she passed us by, we all sat down again. Horse #10 and #11 in line entered, both abnormally high-stepping *big lick* horses. The crowd turned from us and the wild applause thundered across the arena again.

"This is why it is so hard to catch the sorers," Fiora said, her voice seething with anger. "They all support this, the ignorant $$#%^^&**!!!"

"Running walk," the announcer's voice blared over the sound system.

The horses responded immediately, with their heads bobbing, and the praying mantis walk. The riders' backs were all hunched over, leaning forward. I guess that must have been to help the horse from falling over backwards with the ridiculous shifting of their weight over the rear haunches to achieve the impossible high hooves in the front.

"Canter, please," the announcer called out.

The only thing I had ever seen a horse do more tortuous than the *big lick* running walk was the canter. They appeared to be in slow motion. The front legs reached for the moon, and their rear legs crouched even lower. It almost looked like they were rearing, but then springing forward with each small rear. I could not believe they were able to maintain that gait long without intense pain.

"The poor things," Bella said, covering her face.

In contrast, Horse #9 cantered by us slowly, but with a normal stride. Fiora again leapt to her feet, followed by the rest of us, wildly clapping and cheering. Even the judge glanced at us then.

When we sat back down, Fiora grinned at me. She held up her fist, and knocked it against mine.

"Reverse, and line up at the center of the ring," said the announcer.

The eleven horses all slowly turned, and all but #9 walked with the tortuous high step to the center of the ring while the crowd exploded. While the horses stood, Mick nudged me.

"Look at #2, Mortis' horse."

I followed his finger. The back left leg of the horse was splayed, slightly to the side. It trembled, and then moved further out from under him.

"He's having trouble standing," Dr. Creola said.

The announcer was telling the crowd the name of each horse, rider, trainer, and owner in the line-up. He didn't even pause, when

Horse #2 crumpled to the ground and flopped to his side. The rider jumped off, stood beside the poor horse, and kicked it.

I jumped up, shouting, "Hey! Stop!!"

The announcer continued listing the credentials of each horse as though nothing had happened. The judge's assistants rushed over, as the rider pulled on the horse's reins. With a groan, the horse stood. No one asked the rider to walk his horse out of the ring. No vet came running to examine the horse. For a moment, I thought the rider was going to remount. The judge's assistant spoke to him, and apparently put the kibosh on that foolishness. Dr. Creola was already out of his seat, and heading down to the gate.

The top four winners were announced. I almost fainted when Mortis' fallen horse was awarded second place. Predictably, #9, the one unsored horse in the group, won no ribbon.

By now, as the horses began filing out, Dr. Creola was at the gate.

"Look!" Mick said, pointing, "USDA inspectors!"

"How do you know?" I asked.

"Look at Dr. Creola."

He was standing with the inspectors, but looking at us, giving us a thumbs-up with a huge grin on his face. The inspectors wore navy blue shirts, and khaki pants. Three of them met the riders as they came out of the ring. One by one, the horses followed the inspectors to a side ring, including #2, Bob Mortis' horse. Bob Mortis did not look happy.

"They came!" Fiora said, her voice quivering.

Bella smiled at me, and shifted her eyes upward when I looked over.

God again? I mouthed.

She nodded. *God again.*

We watched from our seats as Dr. Creola followed the inspectors and line of horses. We saw him pull aside one of the inspectors, and point at Mortis' horse.

"He's telling them about Sheridan, I bet," Mick said.

I nodded, suspecting that was likely the case. None of us spoke as each horse was led around the cones, and then the pasterns and hooves examined one by one. The #2 horse refused to move. He was finally making his stand. Funny how it came on the tail of him being *unable* to stand.

"He'll be on the way to the slaughter-house auction tomorrow," Fiora said with disdain.

The next class was announced. We huddled in our seats, awaiting Dr. Creola's return.

He smiled broadly when he found his way back to his seat. "Every horse but one was disqualified for soring. Guess who the champion of the class was?"

We didn't need to guess. Down by the inspector ring, the rider of horse #9 was looking straight at us, holding up a blue ribbon and pointing to us.

Fiora stood and saluted her. We all stood, and did the same, following Fiora's lead. Mick shot a look at Fiora, and nodded to her. I was surprised by his expression. It wasn't the slack look of unbridled lust. It was of respect, and even admiration. I know because that is exactly what I was feeling as I hugged her.

Chapter Eighteen

If I had $300 more, I would have hurried over to the farm that owned Mortis' horse and bought the poor creature that had soldiered on so bravely at the show. Dr. Creola told me that horse was so badly hurt that he didn't know if it would survive. It could barely walk when led out of the ring. He suspected that Bob Mortis having had little training time had used more extreme measures to increase the results as quickly as possible. The horse had been sored by other trainers, before Mortis got a hold of him. His future looked grim.

The good news was that every single trainer was fined, except of course, the trainer of Horse #9. Every one had scarring, that we hoped would forever disqualify the horses from showing again.

"They'll just get sneakier next time with their other horses," Fiora said. "But at least they won't be in the Celebration show in Shelbyville. Not with those horses."

Dr. Creola told me that the government inspectors had shown up based on the pictures of Sheridan I had provided, along with his written testimony of the damage Mortis had inflicted. The USDA knew the industry inspectors would be there, and knew issues "might be overlooked." There was a good bit of controversy over whether the industry inspectors were honest in their appraisals. There was no doubt they came up on record with less infractions than the USDA inspectors. Anyway about it, this time, the government inspectors decided based on the evidence we'd provided that they ought to investigate themselves.

They also knew of Fiora's father, and past suspicions raised regarding the horses he trained. There had been some anonymous tips regarding him as well. I was pretty sure I knew who Miss Anonymous was.

It was a major coup for anti-soring, Dr. Creola told me, "And if you hadn't pursued this, I doubt it would have happened." Fiora high-fived me, and even Mick patted my back.

We left the show immediately afterwards. None of us had the heart to watch another moment. As we were finding our way out in the midst of the crowd, someone snatched Fiora's arm. She was right in front of me, so I almost bumped into her as she skidded to a stop.

I didn't need to ask who it was. He had fiery red hair, and eyes of the same shade of blue as Fiora's. She swung around, and when she saw him, flinched. The others walked on, unaware of Mr. Heller's appearance.

"Don't ever come near my home again," he said.

"Don't worry. It is the last place I'd go near."

She jerked her arm from his grip, and stomped away. Mr. Heller looked at me as I sprinted after her. His eyes were full of hatred, deep fires of anger.

Dr. Creola drove us all back to Burton's farm. Fiora was silent, saying nothing to the others about Mr. Heller grabbing her. I would tell Bella later. I thought Mr. Temple would need to know. Those venomous eyes had sent shivers all over me.

Bella and Fiora headed back to the Temple's house. Mick was immediately accosted by Milly and told to saddle up for a trail. Dr. Creola recapped our adventure for Milly. I was left alone, for which I was grateful. Time to go chat with Gidget.

But first, I would tell Sheridan. He was loose in the round pen, which was typical of most afternoons now. Burton told me that one day, I could turn him out in the far back fenced pasture, where Tipper, the old stallion, had been allowed brief field time. We needed Dr. Creola's assurance that Sheridan was ready for that. I hoped it would happen soon. I know he liked being in the company of Gidget. Horses are herd animals, after all. They aren't meant to be isolated.

I slipped into the ring with Sheridan. He stood along the fence nearest to the side pasture, gazing at the only horse in sight.

Gidget. I petted his neck and offered him some carrots, while telling him about our adventures. He listened, but never took his eyes off of Gidget.

"Bob Mortis finally got a little of what he deserved," I said stroking Sheridan's soft muzzle, "The fine is *nothing* compared to what he did to you, and to other horses, but it's a start."

Sheridan gazed placidly at me, his warm brown eyes unblinking. I think he was more willing than me to let bygones be bygones.

"Vicky!" Milly called, "We have a big trail. Would you mind following on Gidget?" I gave her a thumbs up, and scratched Sheridan's forehead.

"See ya later, buddy."

After snagging a lead rope from the tack room, I skipped across the pasture to Gidget. Just for fun, I practiced cantering with the crazy high gait of the sored horses. Unfortunately, Mick rounded the barn and saw me. I caught him out of the corner of my eye, and snapped into a normal walk but it was too late. He'd seen me.

"Disqualified!" he called out, "For being a doofus."

Gidget nickered when she saw me, and met me half way across the field. I threw my arms around her neck and buried my face under her mane. Two more weeks till school started back up. The money from trail rides would dwindle, and Burton would be looking for how to cut costs again. Every year it was the same, and every year, I feared for Gidget. This year I feared more than ever, since now that I owned Sheridan, Burton would be less worried about breaking my heart.

And I loved Sheridan. I did. It was nice owning a horse...though not being able to ride him did take a little luster off that shining fact.

Truthfully, he was a great horse, but he wasn't Gidget. Gidget was the horse that had waited all summer so patiently for me. She was the one I'd worked so hard with for so many years now. Finally she was reliable, at least when *I* rode her. How could I lose her now?

I snapped the lead on her, and scrambled (with difficulty...no surprises there) onto her back. For old time's sake, as she walked to the barn, I sang *Somewhere Over the Rainbow*. Gidget stopped as I sang, which is the opposite of what usually happened. She listened intently, and then turned and nibbled on my knee when I finished. It felt like comfort, like reassurance.

"If you're done with the happy little bluebirds, can you get over here?" Mick shouted from the fence, "We are all waiting on you to click your heels three times and join us."

I nudged Gidget forward and we clattered through the barn, catching up to the end of the trail line as they started down the path along the busy Narroway highway. It was a huge trail. All twelve of Milly's trail horses had been called into action. She must have combined two groups, knowing we wouldn't be back from the fairgrounds till mid-afternoon. Normally she liked to keep the groups no larger than six riders.

Mick told me that was in case all the horses died along the way. At least she'd still have some left for the next trail. "We really need some fresh young blood at this place," he said, "But horses don't grow on trees for the picking."

That reminded me again of my hopeless plight with Gidget. Gidget was young, but she would probably never be settled enough for novice riders. Each year, Burton's Farm seemed to be on the verge of complete financial collapse.

Fortunately, all the horses didn't die on the trail, not even one. We returned safely, without incident. Burton was already pulling the flat bed into position behind the tractor. It was almost time for us to load the field horses' evening hay bales. The tired horses clomped across the barn yard.

The riders dispersed. Mick, Milly, Peeper and I unsaddled the old nags, slipped off their bridles, and smacked their dusty behinds as we let them out the back door into the pasture. Matilda mooed, reminding me she needed milking.

As I took Gidget's bridle off, I stood with her a moment in the lengthening shadows. She scratched her head against me, and sighed, a burst of warm air into my stomach. "We'll figure something out," I promised her. She didn't look worried.

I milked Matilda while Mick tossed hay bales out of the loft. The milk hissed against the metal in a comforting song punctuated by the thud of the bales on the barn floor. The barn cats mewed. Long rays of sun streamed through tiny windows, catching dust motes swirling in the air.

So much of our summer had been spent preparing to nab Sheridan's tormentor. Now that it was concluded, I didn't feel nearly the joy I thought I would have. Instead, I felt the rush of summer's end closing in on me. And worse than that, I felt like we had stuck a finger in the dike, but there was a whole flood of water ready to overflow the dam. I was happy a few bad trainers had been caught, but I was not a deluded fool (contrary to Mick's constant assertions otherwise).

The soring industry had powerful incentives to remain in place. The crowd's response during the show had proved that to me. How does one change the world when the world doesn't want to change?

I finished milking Matilda, drifting into melancholy. When I poured the milk into a shallow saucer for the cats, one exuberant tabby hopped right under the stream of warm milk, and was showered in it. She didn't even move. She just opened her pink mouth and let it splash in her and over her.

That broke the spell of sadness over me. The hungry cats settled in a contented, purring circle around the wide saucer. I patted Matilda's flank, and headed out to help load the flatbed.

"I'm worried about Fiora," Mick said, as we sat together on the back of the truck, dangling our feet over the edge. The flatbed bounced and rattled over the rutted pasture.

"Why?" I asked. I had about a million reasons to worry about Fiora, but I would bet money none of them coincided with Mick's reasons.

"Her father knew she was there, and probably knew she was responsible for the inspectors being there."

"How would he know that?" I asked.

"Dr. Creola was with us, and then he went to talk to the inspectors. Fiora's dad saw him."

Oh. Yes. That was obvious. I was surprised Mick didn't point out how obvious it was, and how it was natural my small head missed that glaring fact.

"I worry what he might do to her."

That thought had certainly crossed my mind, especially after seeing his fury after the show when he grabbed her arm. And another obvious worry suddenly catapulted into my brain. Bob Mortis probably had made the connection between the inspectors and Burton's Farm. I hoped we had not endangered Burton's career. He sure could not afford to lose any farrier jobs.

I didn't say anything. What was there to say? After feeding the animals I was in charge of, I decided to stop off at Bella's house. I wanted to see if Fiora was okay, but also, Bella always made me feel better. I was feeling inexplicably unsettled for having just accomplished exactly what we'd hoped.

Bella was her usual reassuring self. She told me that it was often on the throes of great victory that depression set in. "It's Satan's attempt to rob your joy."

Fiora sat nearby listening. I wondered if she was being affected by the daily dose of Bella's optimism and God-talk. How could she not be? For sure she had changed the way she dressed. I never saw her wear the skimpy shirt and shorts she'd worn when I first met her. As far as I know, she had no other clothes, so all she wore now must belong to Bella.

"Do you think Bob Mortis will do anything to Burton?" I asked.

"Burton probably doesn't deal with the farms Mortis works with," Fiora said. "He'll be okay. I know the farrier that used to work with my dad quit when Dad asked him to put bolts in the pads of a yearling, to bruise his feet. That farrier never worked with another Tennessee Walking Horse owner in the state. If you are in the industry, you shut up or get out. But he is still working as a farrier with other horses."

"What will your dad do to you?" I asked.

Fiora exhaled deeply, and shook her head. "I don't know. Something. I just don't know what yet."

Bella looked at Fiora, a soft fondness in her eyes. "You are safe here," she said.

"Only until he figures out I'm here. Which he will. School starts in two weeks. I can't go back you know."

I hadn't thought of that. She could legally drop out of school, but then what would her life be? And if she went to school, Social Services would have to be notified. She had to have a legal residence. If I'd figured all that out, surely the Temples had.

Fiora didn't say anything else. I had a feeling she was plotting. What a mess caused by one evil practice! She gathered the book she was reading, and headed down the hallway, to the back bedroom.

"Here we did the right thing, I mean we had to," I said, "And Burton, Dr. Creola, and Fiora are all in line to get hurt by it."

"Do you know the story of the Good Samaritan?" Bella asked.

"I know we should *be* one. I don't know the details of the story."

"Well, in the story, a man was beaten by robbers and left to die. All the people who you would think would have helped, like the religious leaders, just passed him by. Everyone had an excuse for why they didn't need to help him. But then the Good Samaritan saw him, and knew that no matter what the result, even if it cost more money than he had, he had to help him."

"I don't know if I would have."

"Jesus told the story of the Good Samaritan to illustrate a point. He said we are to be 'good neighbors' to those in need. Just as God showed mercy to us, we are to show mercy to others."

"What happened to the Good Samaritan?"

"It was a parable, a story. It wasn't true, but Jesus never tells us what happens to the Good Samaritan…only that we should be like him."

"Figures," I said, "It makes a depressing story if he admits the Good Samaritan goes bankrupt and dies a gruesome death, starving and homeless."

"God doesn't ask us to be responsible for the results of our actions," Bella said, "Only to be obedient to what He asks of us. We're supposed to leave the results up to Him."

"What if the results are terrible?" I glanced down the hallway.

"Then there must be a purpose in that."

I considered her story. "I never expected to like Fiora," I said.

"No, neither did I. She has a lot of courage. I don't think I would dare to take the stands she's taken, knowing the consequences."

"I don't think she is going to stay," I said lowering my voice.

"I think you are right. Dad knows that too, but we don't quite know what to do. She has already suffered so much betrayal in her life. We don't feel like we can turn her over to Social Services. Dad talks to her every night, trying to encourage her to let us talk with them. So far she's refused."

"So what will you do?"

"Well, Dad applied to be a foster parent. That is almost in place now. They do a background check on all foster parents, and they said it can take months. And he has to take a class. That starts soon, but it is ten weeks long. School starts in just two weeks…And then also, her own father has to agree to place her in the system. I don't see how we can get around that."

"He probably has to believe she doesn't want it. I think he would do it then out of spite."

Bella studied me, her face thoughtful. "That's a good plan."

I shrugged. I didn't know how Social Services removed kids from homes, but judging from what I'd seen so far of Mr. Heller, he was in no danger of winning any *loving father of the year award.*

"The other option is prove he is unfit, and that she is in danger there," Bella said.

"That shouldn't be hard. I mean he kicked her out and didn't even know if she went to the grandmother's house…which she didn't. The grandmother sounds as mean as the dad."

"An apple doesn't fall far from the tree."

I paused, not sure if I should voice what I was thinking. Bella never chastised me though, so I blurted it out. "But you don't really *want* Fiora for a sister…do you?"

"There are lots of things I don't want that God seems to put me through anyway," she said. "But, to tell you the truth, I think I could learn some things about bravery from Fiora."

"You're one of the bravest people I know!" I cried.

"Oh yeah? Then how come I'm still riding a pony who's shorter than my seven-year-old sister?"

That was actually a valid question.

"Well…you are brave in the things that really matter."

She smiled at me. "Thank you. You always make me feel so much better about myself."

Leave it to Bella to reflect her glory on a completely undeserving other.

Chapter Nineteen

Fiora's plight started to eat at me the same way Sheridan's had. I stopped by the Community library on Sunday afternoon, after our family outing.

Miss Scruggs was there as usual. I never went to the library to find Miss Scruggs *not* there. For some reason, it had never occurred to me that was a little sad. Didn't Miss Scruggs have a family that she wanted to spend time with?

"Hi Miss Scruggs. I have a problem that I need help with."

I would never begin a conversation with Mick like that, by the way. I can't tell you how quickly that would turn into a slug-fest to my tender psyche. But I knew I could trust Miss Scruggs.

"Of course! What's the problem?"

"If a child wanted to become a part of a foster family, how could she force her actual father to agree?"

Miss Scruggs looked deeply into my eyes. She frowned, eyes turned down in sorrow, and misting. Suddenly I understood what she was thinking.

"Oh, this isn't for *me*! I am happy in my family…" *Though I wish Wendy would quit reminding me that even if I was a movie star, Gene Kelly would not dance with someone with no rhythm like me. And it would be nice if John would stop grabbing all the Little Debbies before I even finished half of mine. And I wouldn't mind my own bedroom, and new cowboy boots…*

Miss Scruggs patted her chest with relief. "Oh good! I couldn't imagine you would be unhappy with a mother who is such an avid reader!"

Miss Scruggs could never envision an avid reader as anything but the most laudable of humans. That was all she needed to know about my mom to know she was above reproach.

"No, it's for a friend."

"Hmmm. Tell me the situation."

"Well, the girl is sixteen, and her father kicked her out. He says she left to move in with her grandmother, but that was a lie. The grandmother doesn't like my friend and said some pretty mean things about her. They were maybe true…but they were still mean."

I snapped my mouth closed. I tended to give too much information when I was nervous. And I *was* nervous. What if Miss Scruggs reported Fiora to Social Services? She might be compelled to if she knew the whole story.

Miss Scruggs nodded, and tapped the seat beside her, indicating I should sit down.

"Did the father have any idea where the girl went?"

"No."

"How long was she gone?"

"I'm not sure. Most of the summer."

"Oh my!" Miss Scruggs fanned a magazine in front of her face. She looked distraught. "Social Services would take that child immediately. The father could clearly be charged with neglect. Some agencies will take the child in lieu of formal charges if the father is cooperative."

Well! That was good news!

"Dear, is your friend safe now?"

"Yes."

"I won't pry, but I will ask you to be sure she stays safe. You wouldn't want her on your conscience if anything should happen to her."

"No, I wouldn't."

"Whatever happened with the horse?"

Oh! I had never told Miss Scruggs how our story with Bob Mortis ended. I quickly filled her in, and added, "We couldn't have done it without your help."

Miss Scruggs settled back in her chair and her eyes filled with tears. "Well that made my day."

I stood up to leave. On impulse, I asked Miss Scruggs, "Do you have a family here…in town?"

"No, I am afraid I don't."

My face fell. I think Miss Scruggs noticed because she quickly added, "Don't worry, though! I have thousands of wonderful families in my books!"

I nodded, looking around at the full shelves of the library. Much as I understood, being a voracious reader myself, I didn't think it was the same as a *real* family.

"I did have a foster child for a while," she said, "And that's how I knew the answer to your question. I still have my license, in case an emergency need arose. My foster daughter still calls every now and then."

"What happened to her?"

"Oh, she was returned to her parents when their situation improved. I still miss her. She wasn't much of a reader, though."

I smiled. I knew that must have been a sore point for sure with Miss Scruggs. "Well, thank you again."

"The new Black Stallion book just got here," Miss Scruggs said, "Would you like to check it out?"

My eyes popped wide open. I *never* was the first one to snag the new Black Stallion book! Every horse lover in Chazak waited on the library steps when news of a new sequel surfaced.

"I saved it for you," she said, winking.

As I checked out the book, I tucked it under my arm. "Miss Scruggs, I just want you to know, if I *was* looking for a foster mom, you would be first on my list."

She smiled, patting my hand. "And you would be on mine as well, dear!"

The next day, as I jogged to Burton's Farm, Bella was on her way over as well. Usually, Mondays were a day off for her father, following the hustle bustle of Sunday church duties so Bella did often show up on Mondays. She frequently didn't come till the afternoon, however. She stayed to care for Maria while her dad slept in to catch up on his sleep. Sunday mornings he had to be out at the crack of dawn in preparation for two morning services. I had mentioned to Bella that church would be a whole lot better attended if God were not so insistent on early morning services.

"Why are you out so early?" I asked.

"I decided today you could help me learn to ride a bigger horse. Fiora offered to keep an eye on Maria while Dad slept."

I beamed at her. "Which horse are you thinking of?"

"I don't know. Who is next smallest to Skippy?"

We squeezed through the pasture fence and jogged over to the clump of horses, clustered in a patch of morning sun. It was easy to spot the next smallest from Skippy. She was a gentle old mare named Patch.

Bella stood next to her and brought her hand from the withers to her chest. Patch's back was just under Bella's shoulder height.

"Will she do?" I asked.

Bella swallowed. "I think so."

"We'll try her out after the morning chores," I said. "I found out some stuff yesterday about Social Services."

"Oh? How?"

"I went to the library. I talked to Miss Scruggs. She told me that Mr. Heller would be charged with neglect, and that's all Social Service needs to remove Fiora from the home."

"Well, that's good, I guess, but it doesn't solve the problem of Fiora refusing to let us call Social Service. Maybe if Dad had the license now to be a foster dad she would agree, but it could be weeks, or even months. And once school starts, and she doesn't show up, they'll go looking for her."

"Even though she's sixteen? She can legally drop out."

"I don't know. Maybe Miss Scruggs would know that too. But if she drops out of school, what will happen to her?"

We both contemplated the scantily clad vison of the Fiora we'd first met. Both of us had a pretty good idea of what would happen to her.

And then, the obvious solution hit me. Again, probably everyone else on the planet would have already figured it out.

"Miss Scruggs!"

Bella cocked her head, perplexed.

"Miss Scruggs said she has her foster care license! She could keep her at least until your dad is licensed. And then Fiora could go to school. I bet she would think about doing that!"

Bella twisted her mouth to one side, considering this. Then she nodded slowly. "I can ask her...but maybe you should ask Miss Scruggs first."

"I will! Right after I help you learn to ride Patch, I will run over there. I have a feeling she would do it, though!"

At this moment, I felt a strong shove from behind. Gidget had snuck up behind me and nearly toppled me over with her greeting.

"I saw her coming!" Bella said, laughing, "She was listening for the past few minutes. I guess she finally got tired of waiting."

Poor Gidget! She'd had to do a lot of waiting this year!

We hurried through milking the goats, and feeding the horses. We both mucked my quota of stalls. Since Bella wasn't there nearly as much as I was, she didn't have stalls she was regularly responsible for. I kept my stalls pretty spotless, so in no time we were done.

We stopped off to pet Sheridan, and give him some carrots. Milly returned from feeding the animals on the other side of the yard.

"Hello Bella! Nice to see you here so early in the morning! Vicky, Dr. Creola said it would be fine to turn Sheridan out in the back gated pasture. He was here yesterday, and said he sees no reason for any restrictions on Sheridan at this point."

That was great news! I grabbed a lead rope for Sheridan, and handed a halter and lead for Patch to Bella.

"We'll need you two for the 1:00 trail ride," Milly said, as we passed her on the way out the back door.

"Where's Mick?" I asked.

"He's on a job with Burton. You know, ever since he started working with Sheridan, I've seen a change in him. He wants to learn about Burton's work. He *asked* to go with him today. I know you thought you were just helping the horse, but you helped Mick too taking Sheridan on."

The omnipresent flush of heat bled across my cheeks. Milly often complimented me, but her voice was filled with more emotion than usual. This was very personal to her.

"There have been times," she said, her voice cracking a bit, "That I thought we were losing him."

I understood. The Mick who had so cruelly tormented Joe, the first horse I loved, was not the same Mick today. I don't know how the transformation happened, or really even when. I guess it had been a process.

"Real change usually is," Bella told me when I mentioned my thoughts to her as we led Sheridan out into the pasture.

Sheridan's head was high, nostrils flared, ears perked as we walked across the field. He whinnied to the old biddies, who raised their ancient heads and watched the magnificent stallion.

"I bet every one of them is thinking *if only I were twenty years younger,*" Bella said.

Gidget trotted over and walked with us. I was a little fuzzy on the whole mating thing with horses. I knew a horse came into heat and was receptive to a stallion about six out of every twenty-one days. Most mares shut down ovulation between October to March. Mick told me it was like hanging out a sign for the stallion, that said "Closed for Business" all winter long.

Since a mare was pregnant on average for 11-12 months, that estrus cycle made sense. It was more likely a foal would survive if born in the warmer spring or summer months. It amazed me that horses were designed in such a way that the survival of the foal was increased by when the mare went into heat.

"God again," Bella said, when I voiced that observation.

If I were guessing, I would say Gidget was in heat, based on her decided interest in Sheridan. The feeling was apparently mutual. I had a hard time dragging him into the back pasture. I closed the gate on him, and let him loose. Instead of racing around his unaccustomed field of freedom, he hung out at the edge of the fence, nuzzling and squealing with Gidget.

"I think they are in love," Bella said.

"Now on to Patch." We easily caught the old mare, and led her to the barn. Milly showed us the bridle we should use.

Bella twisted a piece of blond hair around her finger. She kept placing her hand on Patch's back as I bridled her, then measuring against herself how tall Patch was.

"Don't worry," I said. She dropped the twisted blond piece.

"Ok. Let's do this." She followed me out of the barn and to the round pen.

We stopped and I offered her my laced hands to put her knee for a boost up onto Patch's back. "Ups a daisy!" I said, lifting her. She sat quietly, wiggling her hips to settle them in place so they wouldn't come unglued from Patch's back.

"It is much higher than on Skippy."

"But riding will be exactly the same, and you have no trouble riding Skippy. Now just gather your reins, and go for it. I will walk beside you if you like."

She nodded, her face blanched a bit. As Patch stepped forward, she held her breath. It didn't take long before she realized it really wasn't any harder than riding the pony. She relaxed, and breathed a deep sigh.

"I can do this."

"Yes. And you can even follow on the next trail with him."

"You waited very patiently for me to gather my courage," Bella said. "Thank you for that."

I smiled gratefully at her. She never failed to make me feel like I was a worthwhile friend. I knew, despite her words, that patience was not my virtue. For example, I knew that given time, perhaps the nasty soring industry would end. Surely, the law and work of the inspectors would eventually stamp it out. But I did not want to wait. It was excruciating to me that so many innocent horses would suffer while the soring trainers continued to make money off of them.

And then there was the patience demanded in waiting for Gidget to be my horse, safe from sale. Unfortunately, that was not likely to happen no matter how long I waited. Not to mention the patience of waiting for Sheridan, the horse I finally *did* own, to be healed enough that he would let me ride him.

"I am getting a lot of opportunities to exercise patience."

"God will bless that. *Be still before the Lord and wait patiently for him; fret not yourself over the one who prospers in his way, over the man who carries out evil devices!*"

"The Bible, right?"

She nodded.

I did fret over the ones who prospered with evil! It didn't make sense that they would be allowed to keep doing all the awful stuff they did. Why did God allow that? Bella had told me that eventually, they would reap what they sowed, and punishment would be dealt according to all their evil deeds. This delay did not seem fair. Not when there were innocent victims suffering while God took his sweet old time to obliterate the bad guys.

"Gidget has been waiting the whole summer for you," Bella said, peering at me. I think she figured I was mentally wrestling with God. For all her devout belief, she never pressured me to join her in her faith. She also never failed to present His word in every situation.

"Well, yeah, she has. But I wasn't doing anything evil. She was waiting for something *good* to happen. Her lover boy was being restored to health."

"She didn't know that. All she knew was that her favorite human was not around as much as she used to be."

I was glad that even Bella noticed that Maria was no longer Gidget's favorite human. The happier Maria became, the less she needed Gidget. I think Gidget somehow knew that. Meanwhile, I guess that said something about my *happy meter* that Gidget was focusing her attention on me. Like she knew I *did* need her for my well-being. I don't know if it was exactly Gidget that I needed, but truthfully, there was a nagging constant hole in my joy. I was always aware of suffering. Always. That robbed me of complete contentment.

"And do you know why she waited so patiently?" Bella asked.

"No."

"Because she trusted you, and loved you. She knew if you required her to wait, it must be necessary."

I cogitated on that as I walked beside Bella. She didn't explain further. She probably assumed I made the spiritual connection she was going for.

I got her point. I still didn't understand how Bella could be so stoic in the face of all she had to endure with her mother's death, and raising Maria in her stead. However, there was no doubt she was happy, in a way I knew I was not. I'd bet the farm it had to do with trusting God no matter what.

"Shall I trot now?" Bella asked.

"Go for it!" I stepped out of the way. Bella grabbed a handful of mane and kicked Patch's side gently. Patch eased into a lazy trot. Bella's gorgeous blond hair bounced up and down around her shoulders.

"Yippee!" she said.

By the time, she'd circled the ring a couple of times, she told me she was no longer afraid. "It was silly for me to be afraid in the first place. I think I *could* follow a trail on Patch."

Milly traipsed back and forth across the yard, gathering trail horses from the pasture, and tying them to the fence. She'd placed Peeper in charge of brushing them.

"We get our chance soon," I said.

The trail was in an hour and a half, Milly told us. That was time enough for me to sprint to the library to talk with Miss Scruggs. Now that Bella and I were devising a plan, I was eager to work out the details. Bella stayed behind to help Peeper tack the trail horses.

Miss Scruggs was speechless at first when I told her the story of Fiora, with all the depressing details. I told her what we needed was an emergency foster mom that Fiora would be willing to stay with until the Temples were licensed.

"We need to talk to Mr. Temple, but Bella suggested you come to dinner this week. We'll have to let you know what day works for him. You can meet Fiora and we can ask her then…if you think you would be willing to do this."

"It would not be only up to me," Miss Scruggs said, "Social Services would have to approve it. However, I cannot imagine why they wouldn't. She clearly is in emergency need of fostering, and I am licensed to do so. You let me know what Mr. Temple says, and I would be happy to meet that poor girl."

"What night would work for you this week?" I asked.

"Oh, any night."

"I will let you know as soon as we talk with Mr. Temple," I said.

"It may be a long shot what you are planning, but I will wait and see how everything transpires," she said.

Now as she smiled at me, her eyes sparkled with a hopeful yearning that I had never noticed in her expression before. Miss Scruggs was lonely. How had I missed that all these years I had known her?

I realized again that sweet Miss Scruggs always returned to an empty house each evening. Of course any night worked for her. She never had a family she needed to plan around.

When I ran back to Burton's Farm, Gidget nuzzled me.

"She watched for you the whole time you were gone," Bella said.

"Thanks for waiting so patiently for me," I said to Gidget, feeding her the coveted carrots.

Then, I breathlessly told Bella about the discussion with Miss Scruggs. Bella listened, and clapped her hands. She was certain her father would agree to the plan.

"And I hope Fiora will too," Bella said, glancing at Gidget who was vigorously itching her forehead against my chest, "Miss Scruggs sounds like she's been waiting patiently a long time too."

Chapter Twenty

Mr. Temple thought it was an excellent plan. We decided it would be best to ask Fiora before springing it on her at the dinner with Miss Scruggs. Mr. Temple said it sounded like Miss Scruggs would be disappointed if Fiora backed out.

Fiora listened to our plan, as the three of us sat in the Temple's living room. Maria was in the corner, coloring a picture of a horse. When we finished our proposal, Fiora sat back, frowning. I was pretty certain she was about to tell us we were idiots if we thought she would ever go back into foster care.

But at that moment, Maria tossed her crayons aside and ran to Fiora. She climbed into her lap, and said, "I hope you say yes. I like having you here to play with."

Fiora, who had received precious little love in her life, crumpled then and there. Her eyes filled with tears, and she nodded at us, while hugging Maria. The dinner meeting was scheduled for the following night.

When I called Miss Scruggs to tell her, she was silent for a moment. Then, finally finding her voice, it was husky, backed with a sniffle or two.

"I'll call Social Services and give them a heads up. I promise I won't give any details. Not yet. We will see if Fiora will have me, first."

Mr. Temple thought it would be a good idea for me to be there, since none of them knew Miss Scruggs. He thought she would be more comfortable if I was there. The next evening, Miss Scruggs was the first one there, a full ten minutes before I came skidding up to the door.

I barely recognized Fiora. She was wearing a skirt, and a flowery blouse. It was Bella's of course, but it was about as completely not *Fiora-esque* as possible.

"You look nice," I told her.

Miss Scruggs sat pertly, in her usual neat librarian outfit of a drab long skirt and button down shirt. Mr. Temple was there, but was uncharacteristically quiet. He kept sneaking sidelong looks at Miss Scruggs. It was the first time I'd ever seen Miss Scruggs in make-up. It was also the first time I'd ever noticed that she was pretty. I think Mr. Temple noticed that as well.

Bella and Maria saved the day, as usual, keeping up a running conversation about a funny event at church that had to do with a mouse running across the piano during the morning rehearsal before services.

Then, Mr. Temple led us all to the dining room, and said we were in for a real treat. Fiora and Bella set out dinner. Bella told us, with pride, that the chicken had been roasted by Fiora. It was the first dinner she had ever made. I wondered if Mr. Heller had been the cook when her mother died, or if they just ate a lot of sandwiches.

The chicken was good! The baked potatoes were not quite done, but no one mentioned that. Even Maria tempered that observation, telling Fiora, "Dinner is delicious! Especially the crunchy potatoes."

Mr. Temple overcame whatever shyness had gripped him earlier, and explained to all of us what the plan would be if Fiora agreed to it. Miss Scruggs had apparently filled him in on her discussion with Social Services. Now he outlined the process to us.

Social Services would work towards suspending parental rights with the father. There was little doubt that would happen quickly. He didn't elaborate but we all knew that leaving your teen in the forest to fend for herself all summer was not optimal parenting.

In the meantime, Fiora could be placed immediately in Miss Scruggs home. I glanced at Miss Scruggs, who had her hands clasped tightly in her lap, and seemed to be holding her breath. When the Temple's license was approved, Social Service would transfer Fiora to his foster home, if that was what Fiora wanted.

We all looked at Fiora. She had been ominously quiet, and I was afraid that the deal was off. I didn't blame her. She was being asked to move in with a complete stranger, even if it was only for a brief period. Miss Scruggs leaned forward, and put her hand on Fiora's.

"I hope you will agree, dear," she said. "I will try to make sure you have a happy home with me, for the short time we will be together."

"Will I have to whisper all the time, with you being a librarian, and all?" she asked.

She grinned, and looked at Miss Scruggs. I knew then she was joking. It was going to be all right.

"Only if we are in the library," Miss Scruggs replied.

"Then okay," Fiora said.

Bella nudged me softly with her elbow. I nudged her back. We had helped bring about a small miracle, and it sure felt good.

"Well, this calls for a celebration!" Mr. Temple said standing up, "I hear Fiora also made cheesecake from scratch!"

Maria whispered to me, "I am not sure I like scratch."

This part of the evening was not quite as successful as we hoped. As Fiora pulled the cheesecake out of the refrigerator, she discovered that it had oozed all over the place and now was a drippy puddle on the refrigerator shelf.

"It's ok, dear," Miss Scruggs said, as we all peered in at the sodden mess. "I have a whole shelf of cookbooks we can check out of the library."

The next day, I told Mick the good news. He was not as excited as we were. "Mr. Heller is a "mean ##$#%%^%&* and will find a way to ruin everything," he said.

I hoped he was wrong. Maybe Mr. Heller would decide it wasn't worth the effort to be vindictive. Bella told me that God could change even Mr. Heller's vicious, rotten, miserable heart. She actually said those very words, but then apologized for her hateful attitude. I silently applauded it, showing the state of my unforgiving soul. I gathered from Mick's spicy description of Mr. Heller that his soul wallowed in the same sorry state as mine.

We had finished our chores and were ready to try Sheridan in the riding ring again. I put the hackamore on Gidget, and she eagerly followed Sheridan to the round pen. We both mounted, feeling hopeful that the last session's optimistic conclusion boded well for Sheridan's behavior this time. Unfortunately, that was not to be. Just like the past two times, as soon as Mick urged Sheridan to a trot, he exploded, snorting, rearing, and almost toppling over in his distress.

I was ready this time, and controlled Gidget before she went ballistic. I dismounted quickly and led her out of the ring. Sheridan did not calm at all, and finally Mick jumped off. For a few more minutes, Sheridan snorted and side-stepped, with his eyes ringed in white. He thrashed his tail, and pulled away from Mick. So disheartening!

Sheridan relaxed almost instantly as we left the ring. "He was worse this time," I said, discouraged.

"Let's try the trail again."

The moment he walked out of the ring, he morphed back into a gentle, sweet horse, following Mick quietly. Mick remounted in the yard, and one would never have known the wild loss of control in the ring had just ended a minute ago. Sheridan calmly stepped to the trail edge, ears forward, breathing calm.

I followed on Gidget. We walked in silence, listening to the four-note beat of Sheridan's hooves mingling with the background chant of the cars along the busy Narroway highway. Sheridan was the picture of composure.

The horses turned off the section along the highway, and trotted up the short hill that bordered the forest where Fiora had spent her summer. It looked like whatever demons Sheridan had been battling, they had shuttled off somewhere else for the time being.

"I bet I could ride him now," I said. "He couldn't be any more calm."

"I don't know how to tell you this," Mick said, "But he is very perceptive of subtle cues. Like from people who are really good riders. He's calm because I know how to ride. I am not sure he is going to do well with...you."

I knew that harsh as that sounded, Mick was trying to be gentle with me. Nothing he said was untrue. "Let me try. If he is my horse, I should figure out how to ride him, shouldn't I?"

We were at the half way point of the trail. Mick stopped and looked back at me. He sighed. "Ok. No matter how hard he throws you, he can't make your face any worse than it already is."

"Thanks for the vote of confidence."

"Just keeping it real."

He slipped off Sheridan, and took Gidget's reins as he handed Sheridan's lead rope 'reins' to me. Gidget started side-stepping immediately. She clearly did not want Mick to get on her.

"Don't get your tail in a wad," he said, tying her to a tree on the edge of the trail.

Then, he returned to my side to give me a leg up. Sheridan was taller than Gidget, and we both knew I would never be able to get on him alone.

It took Sheridan about three seconds to realize he had a different rider, and one who didn't have nearly the confidence or skill of Mick. He shook his head, side-stepped, squealed, and would've dashed into the forest, removing my head on a low hanging limb if Mick hadn't snatched the lead rope in time.

Despite his taunting, I think Mick was surprised it took Sheridan such a short time to figure out I was incompetent. Honestly, I didn't blame Sheridan. Much as I wanted to ride him, I was scared. Fear is transmitted instantly to horses. I hadn't realized

I was afraid till Mick let go of the lead. At that moment, I remembered him rearing, and nearly falling on top of me. I don't know if Sheridan just sensed my fear, or if I had inadvertently cued him with careless leg position, or something else that a trained rider would be aware of.

I quickly dismounted. I knew when to accept defeat. This horse was far more horse than I knew what to do with. I was fine on Burton Farm plebian nags. This carefully trained, spirited show horse with all the baggage of emotional and physical trauma didn't need a clueless yokel at the helm. He had enough fears of his owns. He could hardly absorb the fears of a rider as well.

I did wonder how I had ever been so successful riding old Joe and now Gidget. For some reason, I had never been afraid of them. I patted Sheridan's neck to assure him I had no hard feelings. It wasn't his fault I didn't know how to ride.

"Don't feel bad," Mick said, as we each returned to our original horse, "I grew up on horses. It makes a difference."

His attempt to make me feel better made me tear up. I owned a horse I couldn't ride. The horse I *didn't* own, the one I really wanted, waited patiently for me to mount. We rode silently back to the barn. While I was perversely pleased Gidget hadn't wanted to let Mick ride her, if even Mick couldn't ride her, Burton really had no good reason to keep her. She was of no benefit to the farm.

"Big trail," Milly said, as we entered the yard. "Mick, what do you think of using Sheridan as the lead horse? It's that or Vicky will have to lead on Gidget alone. We don't have another horse available. I hate to send Vicky alone with such a big group. I'd rather have you both out there."

Mick looked at me. I nodded, telling him, "It's ok. You can if you think he will be ok."

Mick smiled as big a grin as I'd ever seen on him. There was little doubt that Mick was in love. *That* was what Sheridan knew and was responding to. In all the years I'd known Mick, he had never connected with a horse as much as he had with Sheridan. In fact, he'd never connected with a horse at all, expect maybe Trinity and the colt he'd trained as a young boy. There was also no doubt that Sheridan had just as completely connected with Mick.

I could say I wasn't jealous but we all know that would be a big, fat lie. I felt like a new wife whose husband runs off with the wedding planner. Still, part of me cheered for Sheridan's victory over such a formidable foe as Mick's tiny, cold heart. It was no small feat to wiggle into that tight space.

Sheridan led his first trail group like a pro. He was far more energetic than the other horses, and I worried that Mick would lose control. Sheridan pranced, and sometimes side-stepped. I have to admit that through it all, Mick was masterful on him.

I had seen Mick ride thousands of times, but I had never seen him on a spirited horse. He had always amazed me with how easily he stuck to the back of any horse, no matter how much they bounced, or bucked, or even reared. But I had never really seen him ride the way he rode Sheridan.

If you have ever seen a great rider, you know what I mean. Every move the rider makes is in communion with the horse. It is almost like they are a piece of the same body. It really was awe inspiring watching Mick and Sheridan. Mick's slightest movements seemed to be instantly transmitted, and Sheridan responded without me even being aware of what Mick had done to cue him.

He showed off a little, since they both were having so much fun. Normally, Mick just plodded lazily along at the front of trail groups, shouting veiled insults, and bored out of his skull. With this group, he rode back and forth up and down the line, chatting with each rider, and get this, *praising and encouraging them.*

The flaw in his shenanigans was that a clueless novice rider was at times left in front, leading the group. However, it turned out to be the highlight of that lead rider's life. He said he had only ridden a few times before, and never had he been the first one in line. He couldn't wait to tell his wife who had recently complained about how he never took charge.

Mick did have to chase down one brief runaway when one of the old biddies decided she might like to return to the barn. Mick skillfully overtook the old horse, and grabbed her reins. Sheridan looked like he'd been a cowpony his whole life. His eyes shown with excitement, as he streaked alongside the old mare, and Mick leaned over snatching her reins. Sheridan stopped on a dime, swinging in front of the old mare, who knew when she'd been outdone. The rider was effusive in her thanks. Sheridan pranced back to the front of the line, his gorgeous silky tail streaming behind him.

"He looks like a champion," the rider in front of me said, "I wonder how this dumpy farm snagged him." I don't think the rider realized I could hear him. I was miffed that he was calling my refuge on earth a dump, but I understood that beauty is in the eye of the beholder.

The brief episode with the runaway mare was the only minor blip in the whole trail ride. We returned with thirteen unscathed riders, all happy, and all promising to return. Milly and Burton stood together watching us ride back into the barn yard. Mick was perched like a movie star, handsome and confident, on the prancing majestic Sheridan. I could have cried with how perfect they looked together.

We unsaddled the horses, and led them one by one to the watering trough. Peeper scampered from the goat pen to help unbridle and lead the old horses through the barn out to the pasture. Mick led Sheridan back to his stall, and then brushed him (!) and fed him some treats. He was still in the stall, petting Sheridan's neck when I walked by with Gidget, on our way out the back barn door.

Gidget and I paused for a moment, as we always did, before parting ways. I scratched her behind her ears. She leaned into my chest, lowering her head so I could reach her better in all the itchy places. "You are becoming a mighty good trail guide horse," I told her. She nodded, right on cue.

When I returned to the barn, Milly and Burton were sitting on a hay bale. They were talking together in low murmurs. Mick ducked out of Sheridan's stall. Evening chores awaited us.

"We have something we'd like to ask you," Burton said.

Mick and I stopped together in front of them.

"We are wondering if you would be willing to let us use Sheridan for stud."

"I told you I would," I said, "In exchange for the stall." I wondered who the lucky mare was. What a surprise that word of our gorgeous Tennessee Walking Horse had already leaked out.

"Well the thing is, we were hoping to ask your permission to breed *your* horse."

I was confused. Sheridan *was* my horse. But then the light dawned. It always takes me time to piece together clues. Everyone referred to Gidget as *my* horse. I was just confused since Sheridan really *was* my horse, and he couldn't breed himself. (I vaguely recalled that there were earthworms that could do that, but not horses.)

"You want to breed Gidget?" I asked.

"I promised Mick a foal," Burton said, shrugging. "If it's okay with you. I thought I ought to keep that promise."

Mick turned to gaze at his father in wonderment. He had clearly not known of this plan. Now it was his turn to bat back tears.

"And this farm could use some young horses. The old grey mares just ain't what they used to be."

Milly smiled at Burton's little joke, and squeezed his hand.

"But we have one other request."

I nodded, waiting. Mick leaned against the wall, overcome with the thought of raising a foal. He was still blinking furiously. I recognized all the signs of holding back a deluge.

"We're wondering if you would consider a trade."

A trade? I had nothing to trade. No one wanted my frizzy hair though I would have gladly traded it for Bella's golden locks. Same with my pin head or oversized thighs. I had nothing anyone would consider in exchange for those. What else did I have to offer?

"Would you trade Sheridan for Gidget?"

I looked at them in confusion. I was so befuddled I didn't even blink. Then, as though awakening from a dream, one I had been in the midst of for a very long time, I understood.

"You mean...you take Sheridan, and Gidget would be... mine? My own horse?"

"We'd keep the foal, if she conceives, but yes. That's what we mean. Mick can use Sheridan as a trail guide. We hadn't really expected him to be as sound as he appears. And no one but you can ride Gidget anyway. It would be hard for us to keep her unless you wanted her. It would sure make sense, if you'd be willing."

Now I was the one batting back tears. All the years I'd waited, wanting first Joe, and then Gidget. All the books I'd read, pretending *I* was the little girl riding the horse of her dreams. All the stories I'd made up, playing with my little plastic horse statues where I saved each one, and loved each one despite a harsh world that was forever mistreating them. All the times I'd ridden my bicycle, pretending it was the horse I had always wanted, feeling the wind in my hair as I pedaled furiously, and pretended I was cantering on a real horse across a green field speckled with wild violets. All the dollars I'd saved thinking one day I would buy a horse, knowing I couldn't possibly afford a horse. Nonetheless, I'd tucked the dollars away week after week, month after month, year after year.

"Well, are you going to answer anytime this decade?" Mick asked.

"Yes! Yes! But, how much will board be?"

"We will cover board as long as you continue leading the trails in the summer and the classes in the winter," Burton promised. "I don't have a spare stall anymore, but we can build a lean-to in the pasture. Gidget's always been a field horse, and never seemed to mind. If a standing stall opens up, she can have it."

"What about farrier bills? How much will that be?"

"You are in luck. I know a good farrier who will waive charges for you," Milly said, gripping Burton's arm. He nodded.

"Any other deal breaker you want to come up with to ruin my life?" Mick said.

It was then that I realized Mick was hanging on my decision. Mick, terrible Mick who hated the horse farm and every old nag on it, had finally had his heart captured by a horse. And now, timid, meek, gullible, me who had endured years of his taunts and insults held his happiness in my hands.

"No. I think that covers the deal breakers." I smiled at Mick, and he grinned his adorable, lopsided grin back at me.

"Well, then we'll shake on it," Burton said, holding out his hand. I clasped his rough hand, and squeezed.

"Now that that's settled, we need to get these horses their dinner." Burton stood stretching. This was normally Mick's cue to clamber up the rickety steps to the hayloft. Instead, he broke open a bale on the ground and headed towards the back of the barn.

"Where are you going?" Milly asked.

"I want to feed *my* horse first," Mick said, smiling.

I wanted to feed *my* horse too, but I would wait till the work was done. I wanted to savor the moment when I hugged the horse that I finally owned. I would wait till the old field horses were all fed, the goats all milked, and the horses all nestled in their stalls for the night. Then, I would creep out into the warm, still, summer evening lit by fireflies, to tell Gidget the good news. She'd waited this long. I figured she wouldn't mind waiting just a little longer.

Other Books by Vicky Kaseorg

Series:
Burton Farm Series:
Joe—the Horse Nobody Loved
Gidget – The Horse Formerly Known as Witch
Gidget – The Horse I Didn't Own
Gidget – The Horse That Waited For Me

The Whippoorwill Chronicles:
The Bark of the Covenant
The Paws That Bring Good News

Non-Fiction:
I'm Listening with a Broken Ear
God Drives a Tow Truck
Tommy- a Story of Ability
Turning Points-The Life of a Milne Bay WWII Gunner
The Illustrated 23rd Psalm
The Tower Builder
Poppy- The Dirty Ditch Digging Dingo

Fiction
The Good Parent
The Well-Trained Human
Saving a Dog

Author's Note

This was an enormously painful book to write. I had known of some of the abuses described in this book, but not all of them. I watched many videos, and read several articles about the abuses of soring, often while sobbing my heart out.

There are many responsible Tennessee Walking Horse owners. I loved watching a video of a show where one horse was clearly not sored, while all the others were. I fictionalized that story in this book, but it was based on a true event.

Everything I wrote about is readily available on the internet. Soring is inhumane, and the trainers who have come out against it quickly admit this truth. The capacity for humans to disregard the suffering of such wonderful, compliant animals is heart numbing.

I pray that my book will open the eyes of those who are unaware of this terrible practice, and compel them to join the outcry against it.

To Connect with Author

I love to hear from readers! Your comments and feedback are a continual inspiration. Please sign up for email updates to my publications at my Facebook author or blog page.

Visit my Facebook page and "like" it for regular updates on new books/writing. I love to hear from readers! www.facebook.com/pages/Vicky-aseorgAuthor/344952178879131

Twitter: https://twitter.com/vickykaseorg

Follow me on my daily inspirational blog at vickykaseorg.blogspot.com

Stay abreast of new publications at my author page at: http://www.amazon.com/Vicky-Kaseorg/e/B006XJ2DWU

If you enjoyed this book, please go to Amazon, or wherever you purchased this book, and write a review! Much appreciated!

Amazon site: http://www.amazon.com/gp/product/B015ANTRMS?*Version*=1 &*entries*=0

Reviews

Joe- the Horse We all Love!

By Michigan Mom on June 16, 2015

Format: Paperback

I loved this book! It is by far one of the best books I have ever read! It is so well written. When you read it you feel a connection to the horse Joe as if you knew him and he was your horse. She also makes you feel as if you were her or her friend and knew every one of the people in the story. Reading this I laughed and cried, felt happiness and sadness. Being one who loves horses and rides them you can understand what she is feeling and talking about. Even if you don't ride horses you can still understand how the author feels. It's hard to tell you the sensation you get from reading this book, until you read it your self. You feel as if you loved Joe just as the little girl Vicky did! That's why you feel the emotions that are meant to feel. I have always been told a good author and make you feel anything, and Vicky Kaseorg did just that! If you listen on to this book on an audio book the narrator does such an amazing job! Whether or not you read this or listion to it on a audio book you will understand what I mean. Kudos to Vicky Kaseorg and everyone else involved in the book to make this book one of the best books ever!

A masterful triumph of storytelling!

By Piccolo Kate on April 17, 2015

Format: Paperback Verified Purchase

Not since I first read The Diary of Anne Frank as a child have I been so moved by a true story. Several scenes reduced me to tears of joy and sorrow. I could so relate to the author's feelings of loneliness and lack of self-confidence. Her relationship with a lonely horse and how both of them are changed in wonderfully unexpected ways is a masterful triumph of storytelling. This book is one of my new forever favorites, and I recommend it to anyone who loves horses or has ever felt alone. Bravo, Ms. Kaseorg!

Vicky Kaseorg

Gidget- the Horse That Waited For Me

Vicky Kaseorg

Gidget- the Horse That Waited For Me